Leonard Nadel/National Museum of American History/Reuters/Corbis

# Immigration

## RESOURCE BOOK

# ABC-CLIO

**PROJECT EDITOR**

Holly Heinzer, *Project Editor*

**EDITORIAL**

Lynn Jurgensen, *Managing Editor*

David Tipton, *Managing Editor*

Kirk Werner, *Managing Editor*

Liza Hickey, *Editor*

Pat Carlin, *Senior Editor*

Elisabeth McCaffery, *Writer/Editor*

Allen Raichelle, *Senior Editor*

Tim O'Donnell, *Consulting Editor*

Melissa Stallings, *Consulting Editor*

**MEDIA ACQUISITIONS**

Caroline Price, *Manager, Media Resources*

**PRODUCTION EDITOR**

Vicki Moran, *Senior Production Editor*

Ann Claunch, *Director of Curriculum*

# National History Day, Inc.

**DESIGNERS**

The Winter Group

Library of Congress Cataloging-in-Publication Data
Immigration : resource book.
    p. cm. -- (Triumph & tragedy in history)
  Includes bibliographical references and index.
  ISBN 1-59884-012-6 (workbook : alk. paper)
  1. United States--Emigration and immigration--Study and teaching
--Activity programs.    I. Series.
 JV6465.I4724 2006
 304.8'73--dc22

2006014913

**COVER PHOTO:** Ellis Island, New York City.
*Photo: Photos.com*

# Contents

*Bettmann/Corbis*

*Associated Press*

## DEFINING MOMENT
## ACCEPTANCE WITH CONDITIONS

# About the
# Development Team

**ABC-CLIO AND NATIONAL HISTORY DAY** are proud to partner together to bring you the *Triumph & Tragedy* Series. We are grateful to the team that developed the series, especially Michael LeMay, Chris Mullin, and Brett Piersma who wrote the scholarly context and classroom activities to engage students in the process of historical inquiry. In addition, we want to thank the staff members from both organizations who provided background content and resources. A special thank you to Holly Heinzer, Caroline Price, and Vicki Moran who spent countless hours in leading the team through the development process.

**MICHAEL LEMAY**
RETIRED PROFESSOR
CALIFORNIA STATE UNIVERSITY
SAN BERNARDINO

Michael LeMay received his Ph.D. from the University of Minnesota in 1971. He taught political science at the University of Wisconsin Milwaukee and Frostburg State University in Maryland. It was during these years that he became interested in immigration issues, particularly the rates of assimilation among immigrant groups labeled undesirable by American society. His first book on the topic was published in 1987 and several more books and articles followed. More recently, he has been studying the effects of 9/11 on American political attitudes toward immigration, particularly regarding Middle Easterners and the border with Mexico. His forthcoming book, *Eagle at the Gates: National Security Issues in the Cycles of U.S. Immigration,* deals extensively with national security concerns and immigrant populations. Dr. LeMay taught political science at and served as assistant dean of the College of Social and Behavioral Sciences at California State University San Bernardino before retiring in 2005.

**CHRIS MULLIN**

SANTA YNEZ VALLEY UNION HIGH SCHOOL

Chris Mullin graduated from the University of California at Berkeley with a degree in Classical Greek and Latin and received his Master's in Education from the University of California at Santa Barbara. Chris teaches Latin, AP European History, and AP United States History in the beautiful Santa Ynez Valley, California at Santa Ynez Valley Union High School. Chris has been a fellow of the Teachers Network Leadership Institute, facilitator for the California History-Social Science Project, and has developed numerous history-related classroom activities that he has presented at state and national conferences. In 2003, Chris was named California Teacher of the Year for his passionate and innovative approaches to teaching history. Chris is dedicated to finding innovative ways to introduce primary source materials into the day-to-day teaching of history. He believes in challenging students and encouraging them to see history not as a series of verifiable facts, but rather as a compendium of open-ended questions. In lectures, he makes a point of revealing his own reflective process, in order to help students hone their own critical thinking skills.

**BRETT PIERSMA**

SANTA YNEZ VALLEY UNION HIGH SCHOOL

Brett Piersma received his B.A. in History and his Masters of Education and teaching credential at the University of California at Santa Barbara. He teaches AP European History, AP American Government, and College Preparatory World Cultures at Santa Ynez Valley Union High School in Santa Ynez, California. He has facilitated the California History-Social Sciences Project at UCSB and is a MetLife Fellow for the Teachers Network Leadership Institute. Brett has also co-written several award-winning classroom activities. His many passions in teaching include designing primary source-based lesson plans, increasing teacher voice and leadership in schools, increasing student access to rigorous curricula, and perfecting the use of technology in the classroom. Among his innovative techniques are dress-up nights for AP European History students that recreate an Enlightenment-era *salon,* complete with period music and debates on the works of Voltaire and Rousseau.

# Foreword

The *Triumph & Tragedy* series explores three issues currently central to American public discourse: free speech, immigration, and nation-building. None of these topics has arisen overnight; in fact, they have been with us for centuries. This is because all three go to the heart of the American experience and our national aspirations: we are a nation of immigrants who dedicated our country to freedom and liberty, within our borders and across the world. Our treatment of our civil liberties, our new arrivals, and our responsibility to other nations defines who we are. As wars, economic downturns, and political upheavals have challenged this nation's commitment to its ideals, these issues have come to the forefront again and again. Each time, they have been put under the lens of contemporary fears and needs. Each time, they have evoked different responses.

Free speech, immigration, and nation-building have all been reinterpreted during the past century under a variety of conditions, for a variety of reasons. In many instances, the results have demonstrated the best facets of the American experiment. In others, they have revealed an unappealing, even tragic, side. These resource books detail the ways that Americans have dealt with free speech, immigration, and nation-building over the course of recent history, for better and for worse. They present pivotal "Defining Moments" that illustrate both the brightest periods in our history and its darkest episodes.

At their center, these resource books are devoted to providing each student with the raw materials to evaluate each issue on his or her own. In each book, the student will find a wide array of primary materials: laws, poems, quotations, cartoons, speeches, editorials, and images. To help students interpret these historical documents and give them a solid grounding in the topic, secondary essays, glossaries, and background material are provided as well. This material, too, has been drawn from a great variety of sources: experts in diverse fields including education, political science, history, and literature.

Together, these primary and secondary sources form the building blocks for sets of classroom activities. These activities are designed to encourage students to analyze primary documents and to use their conclusions to evaluate the ways that free speech, immigration, and nation-building have been handled throughout past centuries. Students are asked to debate, to role play, and to write creatively about the historical materials. At the conclusion of the activity, the students are asked to judge the actions of the parties involved and to unravel the complexities within each issue.

Opening each resource book, you will find a series of essays designed to introduce students to each topic. The first essay is a broad issue overview. The second essay is more specific and chronological. Next, the books present two "Defining Moments" — landmark historical events that illustrate the nature of debate on each topic. Each Defining Moment section begins with detailed background information. Then you will find the classroom activities, with instructions and a list of materials needed to complete them. These materials, primary sources and reference pieces, follow each classroom activity section. The activities are broken down into parts, each one designed to challenge the students' assumptions and lead them to different conclusions. The last portion of the activity asks the students to assess both the Defining Moment and the issue at large.

In partnering to compile the *Triumph & Tragedy* series of resource books, ABC-CLIO and National History Day, Inc. continue their commitment to challenging students with historical material that both celebrates and complicates our concept of the national heritage. By combining quality research with active learning, we hope to bring the excitement of lively history and participatory civics to your classroom.

**BECKY SNYDER**
*President, Schools Publisher*
ABC-CLIO

**CATHY GORN**
*Executive Director*
National History Day

# Preface

For young adults, it is simply not enough to read texts about vital issues at the heart of American citizenship. Like the generations before them, our students are going to grapple with these topics in their lifetimes. They need to prepare by turning a critical eye upon the histories of free speech, immigration, and nation-building. Their understanding of the past will help them to make sense of the present and to make informed decisions in the future. Teaching students to examine these issues as related to the theme of *Triumph & Tragedy* will provide a framework with which to push past the antiquated view of history as mere facts and dates and drill down into historical content to develop perspective and understanding.

Students sometimes learn history fast and without meaning. The discipline is vast, and the current educational climate emphasizes coverage of content over depth. Class design is often determined by time periods and approached chronologically. But without a guiding framework, students are abandoned to isolated pieces of historical information. A theme redefines how history is learned. Instead of concentrating on the whole century or a broad topic, students are invited to stop and analyze a smaller event, a part of the story, and place it in the context of the whole. Teaching with a theme ensures that students are not overwhelmed with the sheer vastness of the field but are invited to look deeply into a manageable portion of it instead.

*Triumph & Tragedy* provides students with a lens to read history, an organizational structure that helps them to place information in the correct context, and finally, gives them the ability to see connections over time. We invite your students to extend their study of free speech, immigration, and nation-building by engaging in active research and presentation.

# Opening
# Doors

# Introduction

Howard R. Rosenberg,
*"Snapshots in a Farm Labor
Tradition,"* Labor
Management Decisions,
Winter–Spring, 1993

# Opening Doors

## Author

**MICHAEL LEMAY**
RETIRED PROFESSOR
CALIFORNIA STATE UNIVERSITY
SAN BERNARDINO

Few issues have had so great an impact on American history as has immigration. No other nation has received so many or such a variety of immigrants. Since the earliest development of laws designed to regulate the flow of newcomers, the United States has absorbed nearly seventy million immigrants from more than 170 countries (from 1820 to 2003, the total legal immigration to the United States was 68,923,320).These immigrants have profoundly influenced the culture, the economy, and the politics of this "nation of nations." The ways in which the various groups of newcomers have mixed and mingled to become the American people makes for a dramatic and compelling human-interest story. History offers valuable lessons to the future, for better and for worse.

Today, an amazing two-thirds of all persons permanently emigrating throughout the world seek to enter the United States. Over thirty-four million persons currently living in the United States are immigrants. But most recently, economic changes, security concerns, post–9/11 fears about international terrorists, and the feeling that the country has lost control of its borders have moved the immigration question to the front burner of national policy making.

# Elements and Factors Affecting Immigration into the United States

Immigration policy is essentially a blend of domestic and international policy considerations. It performs a gatekeeping function, determining at any given time who is or is not allowed to enter the United States. It also determines the total number of immigrants authorized to enter. In attempting to control the flow of newcomers, immigration policy weighs four main elements: (1) the impact immigration has on the nation's economy, (2) the effect immigration has on the racial and ethnic mix of the American people, (3) how immigration flow affects national identity, the composite sense of "peoplehood," and, (4) priorities of foreign policy and national defense (what is now termed "homeland security").

Sometimes these four components work in harmony, reinforcing each other. When this blend of elements informs immigration law for decades at a time, historians label this period an "era" of immigration policy. At other times, these components work against each other. Then opposing forces seek to influence immigration policy by emphasizing different elements. In all cases and periods, however, these four elements are a key to understanding U.S. immigration policy.

The tide of immigration flow reflects the impact of two major factors: *push factors* and *pull factors*. *Push factors* are events such as war, famine, social turmoil, and political upheavals that propel millions of persons to emigrate from their nations of origin. *Pull factors* are those that draw millions of migrating persons to a particular nation, such as abundance of opportunity, a rich and developed economy, and freedoms such as those afforded by the United States.

# The Waves and Cycles of Immigration in United States History

Traditionally, scholars discussing the massive influxes of U.S. immigrants have divided various periods into *waves*. Their criteria are based on the size and character of the incoming groups composing each *wave*. Associated with each *wave* is a cycle of policymaking determining the approach used to control its size and character.

## 1820–1880: THE "OPEN-DOOR" ERA

The first significant wave, arriving between 1820 and 1880, numbered over ten million immigrants. European nations comprised from eighty to ninety percent of this group, dominated by those from northwestern European nations. They are commonly referred to as the "old" immigrants.

This period is referred to as the "open-door" era. Several laws passed during this cycle, such as the Homestead Act of 1862 and the Immigration Act of 1875, were designed to *draw* immigrants to the United States. Newcomers were needed to populate the burgeoning cities, to provide cheap labor for the growing industrial sector, and to push back the Native Americans and fill the frontier in order to achieve the *manifest destiny* of the nation.

## 1880–1920: THE "DOOR-AJAR" ERA

The second wave, usually referred to as the "new" immigrants, arrived during the decades from 1880 to 1920. This wave comprised a staggering 23.5 million immigrants. They came mostly from the south/central/ eastern European countries. More visibly different from the "native stock" than those of the first wave, this massive flood of immigrants touched off a xenophobic reaction that culminated in restrictive immigration laws that marked the end of the second wave.

This cycle has been called the "door-ajar" era. Laws like the Immigration Act of 1882, the Chinese Exclusion Act with its various amendments, and the Immigration Act of 1917 were designed to exclude certain groups of immigrants deemed "undesirable" by a nativist political movement.

## 1920–1960: THE "PET-DOOR" ERA

During the third wave, from 1920 to 1960, the total number of immigrants dropped dramatically from the 23.5 million of the second wave to just over 5.5 million. This wave was also marked by changes in the composition of the immigrants. Europeans made up roughly sixty percent of the wave, with those coming from northwestern European nations rising from over thirty percent at the beginning of the period to nearly fifty percent by its end. Immigration from the Western Hemisphere (Canada and South America) rose to around thirty to thirty-five percent of the total.

The immigrants of this period are typically called the "quota" immigrants. The cycle, known as the "pet-door" era, saw the passage of such laws as the Immigration Acts of 1921, 1924, and 1929, as well as the McCarran-Walter Act of 1952. This legislation institutionalized racial biases and was designed both to shrink the overall size of the immigrant pool and to shift the source of the much-reduced flow back to northwestern Europe.

## 1960–2001: THE "DUTCH-DOOR" ERA

The fourth wave and "newest" immigrants are those who have come to the United States since 1960. Its numbers were nearly triple those of the third wave, and in annual volume rivaled those of the second wave when immigration was at its zenith. During this fourth wave, immigrants from Western Hemisphere nations—especially Mexico—predominated, rising to more than half of the total. A dramatic increase in Asian immigration also distinguished this wave from its predecessors.

This cycle is known as the "dutch-door" era. The laws characterizing this cycle include the Immigration and Naturalization Act of 1965 (amended in 1976), the Refugee Act of 1980, and the Immigration Reform and Control Act of 1986.

# The Waves and Cycles of Immigration in United States History, cont.

During the early part of this period, the civil rights era, interest in social justice resulted in loosened immigration restrictions and recognition of the plight of political refugees. However, the influx of poorer economic refugees in the 1970s and 1980s, especially illegal ones, caused Congress to rethink these liberal policies in the later decades.

## 2001–PRESENT: THE "STORM-DOOR" ERA

The need to control illegal immigration, especially after the attacks of September 11, 2001 are perhaps marking a new cycle, one that might be called the "storm-door" era of a "fortress America." Laws such as the USA Patriot Act of 2001 and the Department of Homeland Security Act of 2002 exemplify the underpinning philosophy of this cycle.

U.S. immigration policy reflects the perceived needs of the nation as they have shifted over time in response to a variety of factors. Those factors include changing economic conditions, the changing nature and composition of the immigrant waves, and various sociological issues, foreign policy concerns, and national security priorities. The shifts in policy reflect a tug-of-war among the elements of immigration policy, which cause that policy to move back and forth along a spectrum with complete openness at one end and total restriction at the other.

Two opposing philosophies compete for supremacy within immigration debates. One is the view that immigrants spur industrial growth, renew national vigor, and provide a desired infusion of "new blood" into the American stock. This perspective is the traditional base for a more open-door policy stance. In opposition to this stance are calls for varying degrees of restrictions. Proponents fear an influx of strangers who cannot, or in their view should not, be assimilated into the nation. "Restrictionists" fear specific economic effects such as depressed wages and poor working conditions, as well as the dilution of American culture more generally. To avoid such dire effects, they advocate restricting immigration.

# Conclusion

Immigration has been critical to United States development. The laws enacted to implement immigration policy have been many and varied. At some defining moments, such laws have tragically or triumphantly affected the flow of immigration. But in nearly every case, they have had unanticipated consequences.

# Sources

Department of Homeland Security, 2004. *2003 Yearbook of Immigration Statistics.* Office of Immigration Statistics, U.S. Department of Homeland Security, September, 2004. http://uscis.gov/graphics/shared/aboutus/statistics/IMM03yrbk/2003IMM.pdf.

LeMay, Michael. *U.S. Immigration: A Reference Handbook.* Santa Barbara, CA: ABC-CLIO, 2004.

LeMay, Michael. *From Open Door to Dutch Door: An Analysis of U.S. Immigration Policy Since 1820.* New York: Praeger, 1987.

Muller, Thomas, and Thomas Espanshade. *The Fourth Wave.* Washington, DC: Urban Institute Press, 1985.

# Immigration
# and Work

# Throughout History

*Library of Congress*

*National Archives/Corbis*

# The Chinese Experience
## Immigration and Work

## Author

**MICHAEL LEMAY**
RETIRED PROFESSOR
CALIFORNIA STATE UNIVERSITY
SAN BERNARDINO

Immigration laws passed since 1820 have sometimes had such over-whelming impact that they are justifiably seen as "defining moments" of U.S. immigration history. Such laws exemplify the theme of this volume; both the triumph and the tragedy involved in immigration policy. Some laws have been so significant that historians refer to them as defining an era of immigration. Scholars have shown that certain groups have triumphed under immigration law: people of many nations, of all backgrounds and ethnicities, have come and built successful new lives, despite any social prejudice or legal opposition they encountered here. But at the same time, immigration policies have sometimes entailed human tragedy resulting from racial biases used to restrict certain groups targeted as "undesirables."

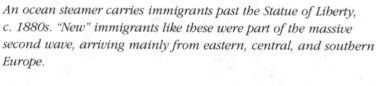

*An ocean steamer carries immigrants past the Statue of Liberty, c. 1880s. "New" immigrants like these were part of the massive second wave, arriving mainly from eastern, central, and southern Europe.*

*Library of Congress*

The flood of immigrants arriving after 1880, when more than 23.5 million people came to the United States, shifted from northwestern Europe to those from south, central, and eastern Europe and from Asia. These new immigrants, visibly different from the native stock, set off a wave of xenophobia that resulted in increasingly restrictive laws aimed at specific groups branded as undesirable. This defining moment in the history of American immigration is one of the darkest.

The first group targeted for discrimination was the Chinese. However, the law was soon expanded to include all Asian immigrants. Ironically, they were barred at the very time when the Statue of Liberty was being erected, a symbol proclaiming the nation's openness to all the poor and oppressed of the world, "the huddled masses yearning to breathe free." The new immigrants caused tremendous fear among some specific groups, such as organized labor, the Ku Klux Klan, and the Asian Exclusion League. The devoted nativism of these groups helped to feed a more general racist fervor.

*Anti-immigration political cartoon from the 1860s.* —————

*Library of Congress*

These groups triumphed in the political process when Congress enacted the first blatantly restrictionist immigration law, the Chinese Exclusion Act of 1882. This law specifically banned Chinese immigrants who wanted to come to the United States to work. Tragically, the term "Chinese laborers" included both skilled and unskilled laborers and those Chinese employed in mining. This law was revised several times, making it even more restrictive, so that, by 1900, nearly all Asian laborers and their spouses were forbidden entry into the United States. Immigration officials used bureaucratic rules to impose harsh measures designed to suppress illegal entries. Between 1900 and 1910, deportation of prospective Chinese immigrants averaged 560 per year. On the West Coast, anti-Chinese sentiment reached its zenith. Chinese immigrants entering through San Francisco's Angel Island were carefully examined, as officials searched for "paper sons and daughters" in an attempt to detect those entering under false pretenses. Chinese immigrants who suffered from the harshly restrictive immigration law carved their laments into the wooden walls of the immigration quarantine station at Angel Island in San Francisco Bay.

*A modern view of Angel Island with San Francisco in the back-* —————
*ground. Thousands of Chinese immigrants were detained and*
*processed here in the 19th and early 20th centuries.*

*iStockPhoto.com*

# The Bracero Experience
## Immigration and Work

In the *Chae Chan Ping v. United States* decision in 1889, the Supreme Court upheld the constitutionality of these racially-based restrictionist laws. The Literacy Act of 1917, the Quota Acts of 1921, and the Immigration Act of 1924 consolidated the triumph of racially-based laws that sought to restrict immigration even more completely than the Chinese Exclusion Act.

After decades of restricting immigration, a series of events led to a profound shift in policy that echoes to the present day. Early in World War II, it became clear that American military recruitment had siphoned off a large portion of available workers. This led to a second defining moment in immigration: the creation of the "bracero" program in 1942. This "guest-worker" program was designed to fill the need for workers by introducing aliens into the labor pool on a temporary basis. Strongly backed by the farming sector, the bracero program allowed migrant farm workers to come to the United States for as long as nine months per year to work in agriculture.

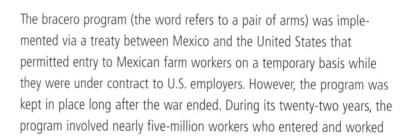

*A bracero program laborer, imported during World War II, harvesting carrots in a field.*

National Archives/Corbis

The bracero program (the word refers to a pair of arms) was implemented via a treaty between Mexico and the United States that permitted entry to Mexican farm workers on a temporary basis while they were under contract to U.S. employers. However, the program was kept in place long after the war ended. During its twenty-two years, the program involved nearly five-million workers who entered and worked in the United States for nine months at a time, most often for seasonal agricultural work. Sadly, as with many immigration policies, there was a dark side to the bracero program. The often tragic conditions endured by the migrant workers were documented in studies showing that the bracero workers were easily exploited.

*At home in their humble barracks after a hard day's work, the workers, called braceros, relax by watching television. The men pooled their earnings to buy the set.*

Bettmann/Corbis

The bracero program was finally phased out in the mid-1960s. Its end coincided with the Immigration Act of 1965, a more lenient law that reflected the triumph of the Civil Rights Movement. The Civil Rights Movement pushed the nation and its leadership to seriously question and reevaluate the racial bias of many of the nation's laws, and immigration was no exception.

Developments of the post-World War II decades chipped away at the quota system. Special acts, nonquota immigration policies, and refugee/escapee laws ameliorated a quota system that was simply too inflexible and too racially biased to be viable. The healthy economy of the early and middle 1960s caused even organized labor to favor a more liberal immigration policy.

But the more liberal immigration trends that began during and after World War II have had distressing and unforeseen consequences. One of these has been a tragic *increase* in illegal or unauthorized immigration. As a result of the bracero program, millions of Mexicans became accustomed to working in the United States. They told friends and

# The Bracero Experience, cont.
## Immigration and Work

relatives that the pay far exceeded what they could hope to earn at home. Workers also forged ties and patterns of immigration that fed the unauthorized immigration flow that has only accelerated since the bracero program was ended in 1964. Compounding the problem, the Immigration Act of 1965, amended in 1976, provided for a 20,000 per country limit on both the Eastern and Western Hemispheres. But 20,000 legal immigrants from Mexico were far short of the demand for their labor, and soon hundreds of thousands were entering as unauthorized (illegal) immigrants. They soon expanded from agriculture to other industries: operatives, construction, personal services, and restaurants, wholesale and retail sales, and domestic and hotel/motel workers. Groups of illegal immigrants have often used human traffickers—smugglers known as "coyotes"—to help them enter the United States undetected. Tragically, hundreds die each year while attempting to illegally cross the border.

# Sources

Calavita, Kitty. *Inside the State: The Bracero Program, Immigration, and the INS.* New York: Routledge, 1992.

Conover, Ted. *Coyotes: A Journey Through the Secret World of America's Illegal Aliens.* New York: Vintage Books, 1987.

Hing, Bill Ong. *Making and Remaking Asian America Through Immigration Policy, 1850–1990.* Stanford, CA: Stanford University Press, 1993.

Immigration Plus. *Immigration and Illegal Aliens: Burden or Blessing?* Farmington Hills, MI: Thomson/Gale, 2006.

Lai, Him Mark, Genny Lim, and Judy Jung. *Island: Poetry and History of Chinese Immigrants on Angel Island, 1910–1940.* San Francisco: Hoc Doi Chinese Cultural Foundation, 1980.

LeMay, Michael. *U.S. Immigration: A Reference Handbook.* Santa Barbara, CA: ABC-CLIO, 2004.

LeMay, Michael. *From Open Door to Dutch Door.* New York: Praeger, 1987.

LeMay, Michael, and Elliott R. Barkan. *U.S. Immigration and Naturalization Laws and Issues: A Documentary History.* Westport, CT: Greenwood Press, 1999.

Nevins, Joseph. *Operation Gatekeeper: The Rise of the Illegal Aliens and the Making of the U.S.–Mexico Boundary.* New York: Routledge, 2002.

Perea, Juan F. *Immigrants Out! The New Nativism and the Anti-Immigrant Impulses in the United States.* New York: New York University Press, 1997.

Sayler, Lucy E. *Laws Harsh as Tigers: Chinese Immigrants and the Shaping of Modern Immigration Law.* Chapel Hill: University of North Carolina Press, 1995.

# A Question
of Economics
and Race

# Defining Moment

Bettmann/Corbis

*Library of Congress*

# A Question of Economics and Race

The Chinese Exclusion Act of 1882 codified racial prejudice toward Chinese immigrants and marked a reversal of the previous U.S. policy of unlimited immigration. More importantly, this act was the first U.S. legislation that did not merely limit immigration in general but banned a specific ethnic group from entering the United States. Brought about by increased overt racism against Asian laborers, the act had many consequences for the development of the Chinese American community and for U.S. society as a whole.

*Library of Congress*

*Chinese laborers work on the U.S. Central Pacific Railroad during the late 1800s. The Chinese immigrants proved to be excellent workers, performing heavy duties and tackling the most dangerous jobs.*

The Chinese Exclusion Act imposed a ten-year ban on Chinese immigrants entering the United States. Chinese laborers were no longer permitted to enter the country and Chinese immigrants who had already been admitted were prohibited from being naturalized as U.S. citizens for ten years. The act was originally vetoed by President Chester Arthur, although he eventually signed the act into law on April 4, 1882, after some minor changes. The act was renewed in 1892 for another ten-year period, and in 1902, the ban on Chinese immigration was made indefinite.

The earliest immigrants to the United States from China were welcomed to the country, but by the 1870s many Americans had begun expressing racist hostility toward the Chinese. Convinced that Asian immigrants were not capable of assimilating into mainstream U.S. culture, many business owners and labor managers paid Chinese workers lower wages and even committed acts of violence against them. Despite their key role in the building of the western states' infrastructure—including the transcontinental railroad—Chinese laborers were treated as near slaves and were the victims of attacks by American workingmen as well as other immigrant groups who accused the Chinese of taking jobs away from them. The act also had a profound effect on agriculture in western states such as California. The exclusion of Chinese workers cut off the supply of cheap labor and made massive single-crop ranches unprofitable, which led to the rise of smaller farms growing a wider variety of crops.

Another consequence of the Chinese Exclusion Act was further development of extensive Chinese ghettoes—Chinatowns—especially in western cities such as San Francisco, Seattle, and Los Angeles. When the 1906 earthquake and fire nearly destroyed San Francisco, the city's federal building and the immigration records housed within it were lost. In subsequent decades, a small number of Chinese men were able to come to the United States as immigrants under a fictional "paper son" status, posing as sons of Chinese professionals who were already U.S. citizens. The destruction of the immigration records thus proved to be a great boon for Chinese immigration because Chinese men claiming citizenship were able to bring their wives and other female relatives to the United States.

*Chinatown after the 1906 San Francisco earthquake.* ———————

*Library of Congress*

In the wake of the new wave of Chinese immigration from 1910 to 1940, a generation of native-born Chinese Americans began the arduous process of gaining acceptance into U.S. society. Still faced with extreme racism and restrictions, this second generation forged strong business partnerships between Chinese and American industries. Chinatowns in San Francisco and New York became more integrated into American life, including participating in public education and utilizing city services.

# A Question of Economics and Race

World War II finally brought the era of the Chinese Exclusion Act to a close. In 1943, with China an ally of the U.S. war effort, the law was repealed with the passage of the Magnuson Act of 1943. Under the Magnuson Act, Chinese immigrants were allowed to become naturalized U.S. citizens, although restrictions on new immigration remained. Chinese immigration to the United States was not granted relatively equal status with European immigration until the passage of the federal Immigration Act of 1965.

*A naturalization ceremony for Chinese immigrants at "China Cove" on Angel Island near San Francisco, 1986. Three new American citizens sing "God Bless America" and wave flags.*

Unlike the earlier wave of Chinese immigrants, who came largely for economic reasons, the 1965 legislation allowed a growing number of educated professionals to enter the United States. Some later immigrants—particularly academics and students—came as a result of China's chaotic Cultural Revolution, launched in 1966. Chinese and Chinese American families were allowed to reunite, and Chinese American communities expanded beyond the boundaries of Chinatowns into the suburbs. In the first twenty years following the 1965 Immigration Act, nearly as many Chinese sought entry to the United States as had done so during the entire first century of immigration.

# Lesson Overview

In this activity, students will explore American impressions of Chinese immigrants of the "Gilded Age," a term coined by Mark Twain to describe the period between the mid-1870s and early 1890s when America industrialized rapidly, creating great wealth for a fortunate few.

Students will need some background in the issues surrounding Chinese immigration and immigration issues of the 19th century more generally.

In Part I, students will read aloud a series of quotes from the 1880s commenting on Chinese immigrants in California.

In Part II, the students will view primary visual images such as political cartoons and handbills on the subject of Chinese immigration, writing answers to guide questions about each one.

In Part III, the students will read two longer articles, one supporting and one condemning Chinese immigration. Using what they have heard and seen up to this point, the students are asked to write letters to one of the authors, either agreeing with or disagreeing with the expressed point of view.

# A Question of Economics and Race

# Authors

**CHRIS MULLIN**
SANTA YNEZ VALLEY
UNION HIGH SCHOOL

**BRETT PIERSMA**
SANTA YNEZ VALLEY
UNION HIGH SCHOOL

# Lesson Plan Part I
## Class Discussion

In this portion of the activity, students will take turns reading short primary source excerpts (Quotes 1–21), which express voice and opinion related to Chinese immigration in the 1870s and 1880s. The Quotes provide both positive and negative views of the Chinese immigrants as well as the labor they provided. The documents have been numbered to create a back-and-forth, pro-and-con pattern. They should be cut into separate placards to distribute to the students.

The teacher should begin this activity by writing down any important vocabulary on the board that could be difficult for the students. Examples might include the following: coolie, Mongolian, monopolizing, Aryan, ethnologists, and Caucasian. Most of the passages are clear enough that a student could read through difficult language and still get the main idea.

Now the teacher should hand out the twenty-one placards containing the Quotes to different students in the class. The teacher should explain that these are real quotations from various people and organizations in the 19th century. The students should pay careful attention to the words as they are read aloud, looking for core arguments and repeated themes, both positive and negative.

The students now begin reading the Quotes in the order of the numbers on their placard. The teacher can clarify any vocabulary or confusing arguments that come up during the reading or wait until the follow-up discussion.

## Activity
### LESSON PLAN PART I

For this portion of the activity, students will need copies of:

PRIMARY SOURCES
• Quotes 1–21 (cut into individual placards to distribute to students), pp. 29–39

Once this read-aloud is complete, the teacher can lead the students in a general class discussion related to the Quotes. The teacher may want to cluster students' responses by creating "positive" and "negative" lists on the board. Likewise, the teacher can create columns on the board that assign statements into categories such as "economic," "ethnic," and "political." The teacher will decide what level is appropriate for his or her students.

Some suggested questions follow:

- What economic arguments did you hear for and against Chinese immigration?
- What positive comments did you hear about the Chinese?
- What negative comments did you hear about the Chinese?
- What legal means of curtailing immigration did opponents of Chinese immigration seek?
- What types of work did Chinese immigrants do?
- In what part of the country did the Chinese immigrants seem to be living?
- What do you think is the primary reason people were worried about Chinese immigration? Is it racial? Economic? Social? Other?

The teacher can lead this discussion in a more casual verbal manner or write down various student comments on the board. Likewise, this discussion could easily lead into a discussion of contemporary immigration issues if appropriate for the class.

# Lesson Plan Part II
## Viewing Historical Sources

In this portion of the activity, the teacher will set up "viewing stations" containing different primary historical sources and some related secondary materials. Teams of students will rotate through each of the stations, analyzing the primary source images (such as political cartoons and handbills) for 19th century attitudes toward Chinese immigration. Each image is accompanied by some background material and guide questions. The students should view the images, read the background materials, and answer the guide questions in writing.

To prepare for this activity; the teacher should make copies of Documents 22–37, each one large enough to be examined at a slight distance, but maintaining as much detail as possible.

The even-numbered documents contain the images, while the odd-numbered documents contain the background material and guide questions associated with each image. It is recommended that the teacher laminate the documents for repeated use and to avoid defacement.

Create eight "viewing stations" by placing a copy of each image and a copy of its accompanying background and guide questions at intervals around the perimeter of the room, in accessible and visible areas suitable for students to work.

To begin the activity, the teacher should divide the class into eight equal teams. Each team should go to a different station.

## Activity
### LESSON PLAN PART II

For this portion of the activity, you will need copies of:

PRIMARY SOURCES
• Documents 22–37, pp. 40–55 (large enough to be read at a slight distance)

Allow the students five-to-seven minutes to study the materials at the first station. Each student should write answers to the guide questions on a separate sheet of paper for credit, but each team should be encouraged work together to analyze the images and answer the questions.

After five-to-seven minutes have elapsed, the teams should rotate clockwise to the next station. Continue rotating the teams every five-to-seven minutes until each team has visited all eight stations.

As a variation of this activity, the teacher can design his or her own alternative tasks or guide questions. Or, even have the students analyze the images "cold"; that is, without the background material or guide questions. Likewise, the teacher could have each team focus on only one station and then report as a group for the rest of the class.

# Lesson Plan Part III
## Class Discussion

Now that the students have listened to the voices of the past and dissected the political cartoons of Gilded Age America, they are going to read two contrasting primary sources (Documents 38 and 39). The first is a speech written by Dennis Kearney, leader of the Irish-dominated Workingmen's Party of California in which he passionately vilifies the Chinese immigrants both in their character as well as in their increasing ability to acquire jobs previously held by Caucasian Americans. The second is an article that appeared in *Harper's Weekly*, a magazine that was consistently sympathetic to the plight of the Chinese in California and elsewhere. In the *Harper's* article, the author turns the tables and paints a degrading picture of the Irish character and organized Irish labor while suggesting that the national government has acted inconsistently and unethically in its passage of the Chinese Exclusion Act.

The teacher should begin this activity by distributing both Documents 38 and 39 to each of the students in the class. The students should read both documents quietly at their desks.

Once the students have completed their reading, the teacher should invite a quick discussion of the documents together. Questions might include the following:

- How does each author deal with issues of race?
- How do the authors present their themes of unfairness?
- What seems to be most important to these authors—race, justice, or job needs?

## Activity
LESSON PLAN PART III

For this portion of the activity, the students will need copies of:

PRIMARY SOURCES
- Documents 38–39, pp. 56–59

The teacher should provide the students with the following assignment:

Today you are going to write a 200-word letter of response to either *Harper's Weekly* or Dennis Kearney. The response letter can support, criticize, challenge, or augment the original comments made by the respective authors. In your letter, you should weave in themes, facts, and ideas that you have developed in the first two activities in this unit. You may take whatever position you like, but you must support it with facts, events, trends, and ideas relevant to the Chinese Exclusion Act period (1880s). In other words, try to write from the point of view of someone living in the period, rather than someone living in the United States today.

# Primary Sources

# A Question
# of Economics
# and Race

# Quotes

## QUOTE 1

The Chinese are rapidly monopolizing employment in all lighter branches of industry . . . such as running sewing machines, making paper boxes and bags, binding shoes, labeling and packing medicines . . . They are . . . used in grading railroads, cutting wood, picking fruit, tending stock, acting as firemen upon steamers, painting carriages, making boots, shoes, clothing, and cigars, tin and wooden ware . . .

Philip Choy, Lorraine Dong, and Marlon K. Horn, eds. *The Coming Man: 19th Century American Perceptions of the Chinese.* Seattle: University of Washington Press, 1994: 84. **Original source:** Henry George [editorial], *New York Tribune*, 1 May 1869.

## QUOTE 2

Chinese labor has greatly developed the Pacific coast. It is in demand and use to-day, and the fidelity, efficiency, and integrity of the Chinese laborer are not denied. Except for the demand, he would not come.

H. H., http://immigrants.harpweek.com/ChineseAmericans/Items/Item082AL.htm **Original source:** "The Chinese Panic." *Harper's Weekly,* 20 May 1882: 306–307.

# Quotes

## QUOTE 3

Men who can work for a dollar a day . . . are a dangerous element in our country. We must not sleep until the foe is upon us, but commence to fight him now.

Andrew Gyory, *Closing the Gate: Race, Politics, and the Chinese Exclusion Act.* Chapel Hill: University of North Carolina Press, 1998: 29.
**Original source:** Andrew C. Cameron [editorial], *Workingman's Advocate*, 6 February 1869.

## QUOTE 4

Without them it would be impossible to go on with the work. I can assure you the Chinese are moving the earth and rock rapidly. They prove nearly equal to white men in the amount of labor they perform, and are far more reliable.

E. B. Crocker, 1867. http://www.fs.fed.us/r5/tahoe/documents/big_bend/rr_const.htm

# Quotes

## QUOTE 5

We oppose their coming because our sturdy Aryan tree will wither in root, trunk, and branch, if this noxious vine be permitted to entwine itself around it.

Andrew Gyory, *Closing the Gate: Race, Politics, and the Chinese Exclusion Act.* Chapel Hill: University of North Carolina Press, 1998: 142.
**Original source:** *Congressional Record,* 45th Cong., 3d sess., 13 February 1879: 1264-7.

## QUOTE 6

As a class they are quiet, peaceable, patient, industrious and economical— ready and apt to learn all the different kinds of work required in railroad building, they soon become as efficient as white laborers. More prudent and economical, they are contented with less wages.

Leland Stanford, *Central Pacific Railroad Statement Made to the President of the United States, and Secretary of the Interior, on the Progress of the Work.* Sacramento, CA, 1865. http://cprr.org/Museum/Chinese.html

# Quotes

## QUOTE 7

Ethnologists declare that a brain capacity of less than 85 cubic inches is unfit for free government, which is considerably above that of the coolie as it is below that of the Caucasian.

Stuart Creighton Miller, "An East Coast Perspective to Chinese Exclusion, 1852–1882." *Historian*, 1971 33(2): 195–196.
**Original source:** Edwin R. Meade, "The Chinese Question." *Annual Address to the Social Science Association of America.* Saratoga, NY, 1877: 17.

## QUOTE 8

Nonetheless, the alliance between the clergy and the businessmen, in attitude if not in activity, contributed heavily to sharp criticism of the clergymen by spokesmen for the California labor and reform movements. Willard B. Farwell revealed something of this hostility in a sarcastic and widely distributed pamphlet:

> The favourite line of argument with the pro-Chinese theorists is that the industrial resources of California could not be developed without the aid of "Chinese cheap labor." That the Central Pacific Railroad was built through the agency of Chinese labor; that every agricultural and mechanical industry has been developed through this agency; and, in fact, the whole material prosperity of the Pacific Coast is due alone to this "blessing in disguise" which a wise Providence has conferred upon this people … The plain and logical deduction is, that if Chinese immigration into the United States is ordained by God; that if it is His will that it should be so, that the heathen many be converted to Christianity, as these fervid missionaries assert, then the opposition to it which nearly the whole people of the Pacific Coast set up is an unpardonable sin . . . and we are in danger of eternal damnation.

Robert Seager, "Some Denominational Reactions to Chinese Immigration to California, 1856–1892." *Pacific Historical Review, 1959,* 28(1): 58. **Original source:** Willard B. Farwell, *The Chinese at Home and Abroad.* San Francisco, 1885: 72.

# Quotes

## QUOTE 9

A population born in China, expecting to return to China, living here in a little China of its own, and without the slightest attachment to the country—utter heathens, treacherous, sensual, cowardly and cruel.

Philip Foner and Daniel Rosenberg, eds. *Racism, Dissent, and Asian Americans from 1850 to the Present: A Documentary History*. Westport, CT: Greenwood Press, 1993: 86.
**Original source:** Henry George [editorial], "The Chinese in California." *New York Tribune,* 1 May 1869.

## QUOTE 10

Why should a nation which did not shrink from three millions of negroes, get into a panic over a paltry one hundred thousand Mongolians?

Andrew Gyory, *Closing the Gate: Race, Politics, and the Chinese Exclusion Act.* Chapel Hill: University of North Carolina Press, 1998: 160.
**Original source:** *New York Tribune,* 8 February 1879.

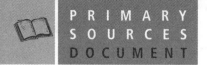
# Quotes

PRIMARY
SOURCES
DOCUMENT

## QUOTE 11

The Mongolians, who are now coming among us on the other side
of the continent, differ from our own race by as strongly marked characteristics as do the negroes, while they will not as readily fall into our ways as
the negroes.

Philip Foner and Daniel Rosenberg, eds. *Racism, Dissent, and Asian Americans from
1850 to the Present: A Documentary History.* Westport, CT: Greenwood Press, 1993: 86.
**Original source:** Henry George [editorial], "The Chinese in California." *New York
Tribune,* 1 May 1869.

PRIMARY
SOURCES
DOCUMENT

## QUOTE 12

We find them organized into societies for mutual aid and assistance. These
societies, that count their numbers by thousands, are conducted by shrewd,
intelligent business men, who promptly advise their subordinates where
employment can be found on the most favorable terms. No system similar
to slavery, serfdom or peonage prevails among these laborers.

Leland Stanford, *Central Pacific Railroad Statement Made to the President of the United
States, and Secretary of the Interior, on the Progress of the Work.* Sacramento, CA,
1865. http://cprr.org/Museum/Chinese.html

# Quotes

## QUOTE 13

The population of this country has been drawn from many different sources; but hitherto, with but one exception these accessions have been of the same race, and though widely differing in language, customs and national characteristics, have been capable of being welded into a homogenous people.

Philip Foner and Daniel Rosenberg, eds. *Racism, Dissent, and Asian Americans from 1850 to the Present: A Documentary History.* Westport, CT: Greenwood Press, 1993: 86. **Original source:** Henry George, "The Chinese in California." *New York Tribune,* 1 May 1869.

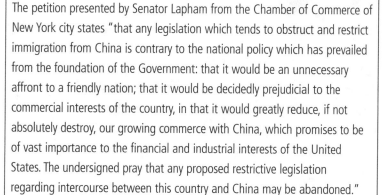

## QUOTE 14

The petition presented by Senator Lapham from the Chamber of Commerce of New York city states "that any legislation which tends to obstruct and restrict immigration from China is contrary to the national policy which has prevailed from the foundation of the Government: that it would be an unnecessary affront to a friendly nation; that it would be decidedly prejudicial to the commercial interests of the country, in that it would greatly reduce, if not absolutely destroy, our growing commerce with China, which promises to be of vast importance to the financial and industrial interests of the United States. The undersigned pray that any proposed restrictive legislation regarding intercourse between this country and China may be abandoned."

*San Francisco Chronicle,* 22 April 1882, p. 3, col. 1.

# Quotes

## QUOTE 15

We have this day to choose . . . whether our legislation shall be in the interest of the American free laborer or the servile laborer from China . . . You cannot work a man who must have beef and bread and would prefer beer, alongside a man who can live on rice. It cannot be done!

Andrew Gyory, *Closing the Gate: Race, Politics, and the Chinese Exclusion Act.* Chapel Hill: University of North Carolina Press, 1998: 3.
**Original source:** *Congressional Record,* 45th Cong., 3rd sess., 14 February 1879: 1301, 1303. [speech by Senator James G. Blaine]

## QUOTE 16

Yet no offense is charged upon these people, and they are but a handful— at most, a hundred thousand. They are not migratory, and they come only because of the demand for their labor. The Federal party sank under the odium of the alien and sedition laws. But they only provided for the removal of suspicious foreign individuals who might be plotting against the govern-ment. The Republican party has gone further in prohibiting the coming of a few honest and intelligent and thrifty laborers. The idea of a Chinese invasion is merely preposterous, and whenever it should threaten to approach, it could be easily averted.

H. H., http://immigrants.harpweek.com/ChineseAmericans/Items/Item082AL.htm
**Original source:** "The Chinese Panic." *Harper's Weekly,* 20 May 1882: 306–307.

## QUOTE 17

District-Attorney Pratt made an extended anti-Chinese speech, in the course of which he said that he hated and abhorred riot and bloodshed, it was his business to pursue and convict for such acts, but when a hard-working man, who was unable to find employment, went home at night and found his family crying for bread, he could not be expected to sit calmly by. If we could not prevent the Chinese immigration by legislation, the time would come when the people would rise up and put a stop to it by force.

*San Francisco Chronicle,* 13 April 1882, p. 2, col. 3.

## QUOTE 18

There is not sufficient evidence of the coming invasion from China to make any restriction necessary. But were there abundant and conclusive evidence, this bill seems to us to violate our treaty obligations, to be needlessly and dishonorably severe, and to invite reciprocal hostile legislation on the part of the Chinese government.

*San Francisco Examiner,* 4 May 1882, p. 1, col. 3.

# Quotes

### QUOTE 19

The merchants have been the last to realize it, but I think nearly all of them understand now that their business is falling off because the laboring [white] men cannot earn money to buy.

Robert Seager, "Some Denominational Reactions to Chinese Immigration to California, 1856–1892." *Pacific Historical Review,* 1959, 28(1): 60.
**Original source:** *Investigation by a Select Committee of the House of Representatives Relative to the Causes of the General Depression in Labor and Business; and as to Chinese Immigration* 46th Cong., 2 sess., House Misc. Doc. No. 5. Washington, DC, 1879: 258.

### QUOTE 20

They are faithful and industrious, and under proper supervision, soon become skillful in the performance of their duties. Many of them are becoming very expert in drilling, blasting, and other departments of rock work.

*Report of the Chief Engineer upon Recent Surveys and Progress of Construction of the Central Pacific Railroad* of California (1865). Courtesy of Lynn Farrar.
http://cprr.org/Museum/Chinese.html

# Quotes

## QUOTE 21

We warn workingmen that a new and dangerous foe looms up in the far west. Already our brothers of the Pacific have to meet it, and just as soon as the Pacific railroad is completed, and trade and travel begins to flow from the east across our continent, these Chinamen will begin to swarm through the rocky mountains, like devouring locusts spread out over the country this side.

Andrew Gyory, *Closing the Gate: Race, Politics, and the Chinese Exclusion Act.* Chapel Hill: University of North Carolina Press, 1998: 29.
**Original source:** Andrew C. Cameron [editorial], *Workingman's Advocate*, 6 February 1869.

# Document 22
## Political Cartoon

THE MARTYRDOM OF ST. CRISPIN.

*Harpweek*

Political cartoon on the subject of Chinese

immigrant labor in American industry.

# Document 23
## Background and Guide Questions

Historically, St. Crispin was a Catholic saint, but in this context, he
was also a real-life Massachusetts shoemaker who imported
Chinese labor to work in his factory.

• What is the primary message in this document?

• Does it support or criticize Chinese immigrants? Explain.

• Give three examples of how the artist uses images to express his
viewpoint.

• Why do you think the non-Chinese shoemaker (Crispin) is
depicted with a halo?

# Document 24

## Political Cartoon

A 1871 *Harper's Weekly* political cartoon depicts Lady Liberty or "Columbia" protecting a Chinese immigrant.

*Harpweek*

# Document 25
## Background and Guide Questions

This image shows "Columbia" protecting "John Chinaman" from attack. The image of "Columbia," a beautiful, noble, Caucasian female figure representing America, was invented during the American Revolution. The name is a feminized version of "Columbus." The symbol has been replaced more recently by the female Statue of Liberty and the masculine "Uncle Sam." "Columbia" remained popular during the 19th century; often used as a motherly protector or a damsel in distress, depending on the issue. Here she comforts and guards a Chinese immigrant. The figures in the background have monkey-like, subhuman faces. Such caricatures had been used to represent Irish immigrants since the late 1840s and would have been instantly recognizable to a 19th-century American audience.

• What is the primary message in this document?

• Does it support or criticize Chinese immigrants? Explain.

• Give three examples of how the artist uses images to express his viewpoint.

• What are some of the powerful statements written on the wall behind the Chinese man?

• How is "Columbia" different from common images of Uncle Sam?

• How are the non-Chinese men portrayed in the cartoon?

# Document 26
## Handbill

# To THE WORKINGMEN
## OF THE EASTERN STATES!
### HEAR YE!

Your fellow Workingmen of California have for years been using every means in their power to get rid of **CHINESE CHEAP LABOR**, but Rich Corporations, the monied men, backed by a Republican Press and President, have crushed all their efforts, and now they lie helpless at the feet of their masters, and can only cry to you for deliverance.

## Cooley Cheap Labor

rules the market there, and will do the same here by and by, if the blow is not struck now. As Holy Writ says: "NOW IS THE DAY OF YOUR SALVATION." Workingmen now is your time to mortally wound the double-headed monster **YELLOW SLAVERY**, and check the growing, grasping power of Corporations.

## Brethren, are you Ready for the Question?

If you hesitate, let me tell you, in words of prophecy, if you don't do it now peacably by your ballot, your children will have to do it by their blood.

A FORMER RESIDENT OF CALIFORNIA.

*New York State Library*

Handbill opposing influx

of Chinese labor.

# Document 27
## Background and Guide Questions

This is a good example of the sort of political "handbills" that were very common among workers' organizations in the 19th and early 20th centuries. They usually encouraged a specific political belief or course of action for workers.

• What is the primary message in this document?

• Does it support or criticize Chinese immigrants? Explain.

• What are some strong phrases describing the Chinese in this document?

• The author uses the word "Brethren" and the sentence "Now is the day of your salvation!" Why does the writer use those words?

PRIMARY
SOURCES
CARTOON

# Document 28
## Political Cartoon

**AT FRISCO.**

"See here, me Chinee Haythun, I'm wan of the Committee of National Safety; and bringing to me moind the words of George O'Washington and Dan'l O'Webster in regarrd to Furrin Inflooince, ye must go. D'ye understand? Ye must go!"

*Harpweek*

Political cartoon depicting a meeting

of 19th-century immigrant groups:

the Irish and the Chinese.

# Document 29
## Background and Guide Questions

In this cartoon, we see a stereotypical Irish immigrant speaking to a stereotypical Chinese man. The Irishman is speaking with a very thick Irish accent. The text without the accent should read: "See here my Chinese Heathen, I'm one of the Committee of National Safety, and bringing to my mind the words of George Washington and Daniel Webster in regard to foreign influence, you must go. Do you understand, you must go!"

• What is the primary message in this document?

• Does it support or criticize Chinese immigrants? Explain.

• Give three examples of how the artist uses images to express his viewpoint.

• What sort of items is the Irishman carrying, wearing, or using that reveal the artist's view of his character?

• Why do you think the artist has the Irishman say "In regard to foreign influence, you must go" with such a strong accent?

• Why does the Irishman call George Washington and Daniel Webster, "O'Washington" and "O'Webster?"

# Document 30
## Illustration

CHINESE MERCHANTS' EXCHANGE, SAN FRANCISCO.—Drawn by P. Frenzeny, from a Sketch by W. W. Bode.—[See Page 174.]

*Harpweek*

Illustration of a Chinese
merchant's exchange in
San Francisco c. 1882.

# Document 31
## Background and Guide Questions

In this picture we see inside what one can assume is a typical Chinese merchant center in San Francisco during the 1880s. The drawing, created by Thomas Nast, a Caucasian cartoonist for *Harper's Weekly*, gives the viewer a peek inside a private community of Chinese immigrants living and working in America. Nast uses a wide variety of images within the picture to clearly convey his personal point of view concerning the Chinese immigrants.

• What is the primary message in this document?

• Does it support or criticize Chinese immigrants? Explain.

• What sort of activities are taking place?

• Give three examples of how the artist uses images to express his viewpoint.

• What are some of the positive things that the writer shows this business provides?

# Document 32
## Political Cartoon

The Bancroft Library, University of California

"What Should We Do With
Our Boys?" as published
in The Wasp, p. 8,
January–June 1882.

# Document 33
## Background and Guide Questions

In this picture we see a multi-armed Chinese immigrant with many hands working rapidly in a wide variety of handicraft businesses. Because of the immigrant's skill and work ethic, young Caucasian boys have been turned away from the business unable to secure a job. Some of the young men are loitering and another is being taken away by a local constable, presumably to some sort of penitentiary. The caption reads "What shall we do with our boys?"

• What is the primary message in this document?

• Does it support or criticize Chinese immigrants? Explain.

• Give three examples of how the artist uses images to express his viewpoint.

• Why do you think the policeman is shown taking away one of the young men?

• Why do you think the Chinese man is depicted as having so many hands?

• Why is the cartoon entitled: "What shall we do with our boys?"

# Document 34
## Political Cartoon

LET THE CHINESE EMBRACE CIVILIZATION, AND THEY MAY STAY.

*Harpweek*

Political cartoon depicting

Chinese assimilation into

American culture.

# Document 35
## Background and Guide Questions

The artist here is poking fun at the claims of so-called "native Americans" or "nativists." A great many critics of Chinese immigration felt that the core values and customs which the Chinese brought with them would ultimately undermine the pure American traditions and character. Here the artist has selected a sampling of unique American customs which are less than desirable.

Furthermore, these are practices which can probably be linked to the type of people that most nativists were themselves. The overall statement is probably something along either the line that many Americans would be improved by a little dose of Chinese culture or that the customs Chinese might be replacing are not so attractive anyway.

- What is the primary message in this document?

- Does it support or criticize Chinese immigrants? Explain.

- Give three examples of how the artist uses images to express his viewpoint.

- What sort of activities does the artist suggest represent civilization?

- Is the artist being playful or serious in his recommendations? Explain.

# Document 36
## Political Cartoon

*Library of Congress*

A political cartoon from

the 1860s is captioned

"Every Dog Has His Day."

# Document 37
## Background and Guide Questions

In this picture we see a Native American, an African American (presumably an ex-slave), and a Chinese immigrant. The caption, "Every Dog Has His Day," is an old expression meaning that even the lowliest of creatures has its moment in the sun. Here it is obviously being used ironically since the conditions visited upon all three of these groups were by no means desirable. African Americans had been enslaved and in the late 19th century still had very few civil rights. Native Americans, because of western expansion, had been violently removed from their lands. Now the Chinese immigrants, so the artist suggests, are receiving equally unjust treatment. One can read the signboard to better understand some of the specific abuses. One of the more ironic references in this cartoon is to the Irish. During the 1840s and 1850s, Irish immigrants had received a tremendous amount of abuse at the hands of "nativists" from previous waves of European immigration. Yet these same Irish were the ones in California so violently attacking the Chinese.

• What is the primary message in this document?

• Does it support or criticize Chinese immigrants? Explain.

• Give three examples of how the artist uses images to express his viewpoint.

• What does the title "Every Dog Has His Day" mean in this context?

• Why do you think there are an African American and a Native American alongside the Chinese man?

• What are some of the writings on the wall and what do they mean?

• Written on the wall is the phrase: "Down with the Irish." How is that ironic based on events in California?

# Document 38
## Our Misery and Despair:
## Dennis Kearney Blasts Chinese Immigration

*This speech was written prior to passage of the Chinese Exclusion Act in 1882. Dennis Kearney, the author, led the Irish attack on Chinese immigration in California.*

"Workingmen must form a party of their own, take charge of the government, dispose gilded fraud, and put honest toil in power. In our golden state all these evils have been intensified. Land monopoly has seized upon all the best soil in this fair land. A few men own from ten thousand to two hundred thousand acres each. The poor Laborer can find no resting place, save on the barren mountain, or in the trackless desert. Money monopoly has reached its grandest proportions. Here, in San Francisco, the palace of the millionaire looms up above the hovel of the starving poor with as wide a contrast as anywhere on earth. To add to our misery and despair, a bloated aristocracy has sent to China—the greatest and oldest despotism in the world—for a cheap working slave. It rakes the slums of Asia to find the meanest slave on earth—the Chinese coolie—and imports him here to meet the free American in the Labor market, and still further widen the breach between the rich and the poor, still further to degrade white Labor. These cheap slaves fill every place. Their dress is scant and cheap. Their food is rice from China. They hedge twenty in a room, ten by ten. They are whipped curs, abject in docility, mean, contemptible and obedient in all things. They have no wives, children or dependents. They are imported by companies, controlled as serfs, worked like slaves, and at last go back to China with all their earnings. They are in every place, they seem to have no sex. Boys work, girls work; it is all alike to them. The father of a (White) family is met by them (the Chinese) at every turn. Would he get work for himself? Ah! A stout Chinaman does it cheaper. Will he get a place for his oldest boy? He can not. His girl? Why the Chinaman is in her place too! Every door is closed. He can only go to crime or suicide, his wife and daughter to prostitution, and his boys to hoodlumism and the penitentiary. Do not believe those who call us savages, rioters, incendiaries, and outlaws. We seek our ends calmly, rationally, at the ballot box. So far good order has marked all our proceedings. But, we know how false, how inhuman, our adversaries are. We know that if gold, if fraud, if force can defeat us, they will all be used. And we have resolved that they shall not defeat us. We shall arm. We shall meet fraud and falsehood with defiance, and force with force, if need be. We are men, and propose to live like men in this free land, without the contamination of slave labor, or die like men, if need be, in asserting the rights of our race, our country, and our families. California must be all American or all Chinese. We are resolved that it shall be American, and are prepared to make it so. May we not rely upon your sympathy and assistance?"

With great respect for the Workingmen's Party of California.

Dennis Kearney, President

*Source: Dennis Kearney, President, and H. L. Knight, Secretary, "Appeal from California. The Chinese Invasion. Workingmen's Address," Indianapolis Times, February 28, 1878.*

# Document 39

## The Chinese Panic:
### *Harper's Weekly* May 20th, 1882

*The following article was written in response to Congress' passage of the Chinese Exclusion Act and in response to anti-Chinese attacks by the Irish-dominated Workingmen's Party of California. The president who signed the Chinese Exclusion Act into law was Republican Chester A. Arthur.*

"The Republicans have taken the responsibility of prohibiting the voluntary immigration of free skilled laborers into the country, and have been the first to renounce the claim that America welcomes every honest comer, and offers a home to the honest victim of the oppression of kings or of cruel laws. Chinese labor has greatly developed the Pacific coast. It is in demand and use to-day, and the fidelity, efficiency, and integrity of the Chinese laborer are not denied. Except for the demand, he would not come. Henceforth for ten years any one who comes may be imprisoned for a year, and then expelled from the country. Those who are already here must be registered, and furnished with passports to authenticate themselves, and justify their traveling in the country. Chinese travelers who are not laborers nor residents will be admitted to the country only by passports, and the national and State governments are prohibited from naturalizing any Chinese person. Yet no offense is charged upon these people, and they are but a handful—at most, a hundred thousand. They are not migratory, and they come only because of the demand for their labor . . . The idea of a Chinese invasion is merely preposterous, and whenever it should

threaten to approach, it could be easily averted. Having laid down the
principle of discrimination against foreign immigration, those who are
responsible for it ought not to shrink from the just consequences."

"The statistics of crime and disorder in the country and the records of
corruption in our politics show that all of them have been greatly
increased and stimulated by the Irish immigration. Dangers to the free-
school system have also appeared from the same source. Threatening
complications with friendly foreign states are due to the same element.
Why not suspend the Irish immigration for ten years, and imprison the
honest Irishman who comes of his own free will to get higher wages
and to improve his condition? Why not require all those who are
already here to obtain certificates from the collectors of ports, and to
produce passports if they wish to move about the country? Why not
enact that Irishmen who are not laborers shall be admitted to the
country only with passports, and that the words "Irish laborers" shall
be construed to mean both skilled and unskilled laborers? Why not, but
that such provisions would be repugnant to the American principle and
to common-sense? Yet such an exclusion would be very much more
plausible than that of the Chinese."

*Source:* Harper's Weekly *editorial, May 20, 1882, 306–307.*

# Glossary Words, Ideas, or Movements
A Question of Economics and Race

**ANTI-IMMIGRATION MOVEMENT** Immigration in the United States has met with vigorous opposition since the time of Benjamin Franklin (some would even say since Jamestown). Franklin said that the German immigration of "Palatine Boors" would alter the character of the United States because they could not be assimilated. Large-scale immigration to the United States, beginning after the Civil War, consisted of people from southern and east central Europe, and twenty-seven million came between 1870 and 1920. Unlike the earlier immigrants from Germany and the British Isles, these were fundamentally different from the Anglo-Saxon norm. Anti-immigration activists sought to keep certain classes or races of people out of the United States, fearing that the Anglo-Saxon culture of the country would dissolve in the influx of new cultures. Racism, anti-Catholicism, and anti-Semitism were all part of this movement.

Anti-immigration advocates were mostly native-born white American Protestants and were extremely xenophobic. They achieved some early successes in Congress with legislation that barred non-European races, "polygamists" (which could be interpreted to mean people from India and the Muslim world), and "anarchists" from entering. The Chinese were barred from U.S. citizenship even when they had entered the nation legally. Anti-immigration zealots such as Lothrop Stoddard heaped scorn upon the newcomers who did arrive, calling Greeks "the scum of Europe" and asserting that Italians were "mulattoes" because of the Moorish conquest of Italy centuries earlier. There was a strong element of pseudo-scientific racism in the speeches of the anti-immigration movement.

To justify their intolerance, anti-immigration activists insisted that immigrants could not be assimilated, that they would be disloyal to the U.S. if they achieved citizenship. These attitudes led to attempts to "Americanize" immigrants with citizenship classes, literacy classes, and even cooking classes. The Department of Labor's *Textbook for Students*, written by immigration educator Raymond Crist in 1918, starts with basic English vocabulary and moves on to American history, government, and household hints.

Ultimately, all immigrants assimilated to some degree. Some, such as the Scandinavians became completely Anglo-Saxonized, whereas Italians and Greeks often retained some cultural practices such as holding church festivals and cooking ethnic foods.

The Quota Acts of 1921 and 1923 ended most southern, central, and eastern European immigration; anti-immigration workers described them as "Victory in the Twenties." The Acts limited each nationality to an annual immigration of three percent of its population already in the United States. Assimilation proceeded for the immigrants who did arrive, as immigrant families were surrounded by Americans, and children grew up Americanized. With the ebbing of immigrant newspapers and societies as the decades passed, the anti-immigration movement also faded. In the 1980s and 1990s, however, far-right political figures such as Pat Buchanan called for renewed restrictions on immigration, especially given increased illegal immigration from Mexico and Cuba. Although new restrictions seem unlikely, the debate over immigration continues.

# Glossary Words, Ideas, or Movements
## A Question of Economics and Race, cont.

**ARYAN** A term used to describe a group of people who, in prehistoric times, lived in Iran and northern India. They were traditionally very light-skinned, so the term "Aryan" became synonymous with "white."

**CAUCASIAN** In the 19th-century United States, this term denoted persons with light skin, descended mainly from northwestern Europeans. Caucasians were considered to be a distinct white race.

**CELESTIAL** An outdated ethnic term for "Chinese," probably originating in the fact that the historic symbol of China was the "celestial dragon" and the nation was known as the "Celestial Empire."

**COOLIE/COOLEY** A derogatory term for an unskilled laborer from Asia who was willing to work abroad for low pay during the 19th century. It was commonly used in the United States by whites when referring to the Chinese laborers who worked on the transcontinental railroad or took domestic jobs such as gardener, housekeeper, or launderer.

**ETHNOLOGIST/ETHNOLOGY** Anthropologist who studies the origin and development of human races and ethnic groups; this field is known as ethnology.

**"GOLD MOUNTAIN"** "Gum San" in Chinese. This was the term prospective Chinese immigrants used to describe California after the discovery of gold there in 1848.

**GROG** Rum diluted with water, sometimes with lime juice and sugar added. This drink was served to sailors from the 17th through the 19th centuries.

**HOMOGENOUS** Uniform; all of one kind.

**MONGOLIANS** A term referring to the Chinese in general, though the term "Mongol" actually refers to a specific group of nomadic people who live in Mongolia, the borderland region between Russia and China.

**MONOPOLY/MONOPOLIZE/MONOPOLIST** A company that is the only firm supplying a product or service to a market. Monopolies have no competitors, which allows them to set prices and terms without any constraints. They defeat the ideals underlying a market economy.

**"PAPER SONS" AND "PAPER DAUGHTERS"** Terms that refer to a deception that was used by 19th-century Chinese immigrants trying to enter the United States illegally. Because a child of an American citizen was automatically an American citizen, Chinese immigrants would buy false papers claiming that they were the children of citizen fathers: they were "paper sons" or "paper daughters." This practice resulted in extremely detailed interrogations by immigration officials on Angel Island. The process for admittance was slowed down considerably as administrators tried to uncover false claimants.

**SERFDOM/PEONAGE** A form of slavery, except that the persons are tied to property, rather than being owned outright by another human being. Serfs are peasants who are bound to the land that they work. Peons are traditionally people who are bound to work off a debt—free once they have worked a sufficient amount.

**SERVILE** Behaving like a slave or servant.

# Biographies and Organizations
## A Question of Economics and Race

*Library of Congress*

### ARTHUR, CHESTER A.

Chester A. Arthur was born in Vermont in 1829. He attended Union College and passed the bar in New York before serving as a militia officer during the Civil War. Elected vice president in 1880, Arthur became the twenty-first president of the United States when James Garfield was assassinated in 1881. Arthur left office in 1884, after the Republican Party failed to nominate him for his own term, and died in 1886.

President Arthur was intensely loyal to the Republican Party; this won him the vice presidential spot on the 1880 ticket. However, he did break with his contemporaries on some key points, especially by backing civil service reform and lowering duties on foreign imports. He also stood aside from his congressional allies and much of the nation on the Chinese Exclusion Act. Arthur believed that Chinese labor was important to national development, especially in building and maintaining railroads. He feared that the Chinese government would retaliate by refusing to trade with the United States. However, when the bill was amended, lowering the period of exclusion from twenty years to ten, Arthur gave in and signed the act into law.

### "BIG FOUR"

Charles Crocker, Mark Hopkins, Collis P. Huntington, and Leland Stanford were known collectively as the "Big Four." These men owned the Central Pacific Railroad and spearheaded the construction of the western portion of the transcontinental railway. As a result, they acquired a near-monopoly of the California transportation system. Their wealth and power allowed them to control the state's politics as well. There were some unsuccessful attempts to curtail the Big Four's reach, such as a new state constitution written in 1879, but they held on into the early 20th century.

*Courtesy of the Bancroft Library*

## KEARNEY, DENNIS

Founder of the Workingmen's Party of California. Kearney was an Irish immigrant who led the anti-Chinese movement on the West Coast. Established in 1877, his party had a single slogan "The Chinese Must Go!" Kearney did not back away from advocating violence and was briefly jailed for disturbing the peace. He and the Party urged Congress to bar Chinese immigration, saying that white Americans were being denied jobs and that Chinese labor depressed wages. His arguments were based partly on labor issues, partly on racism.

## NAST, THOMAS

The most important political cartoonist in 19th-century America, known for exposing government corruption.

*National Archives*

## STANFORD, LELAND

The best known of the "Big Four," the businessmen who essentially ran California in the late 19th century. Leland Stanford was born on March 9, 1824, in Watervliet, New York. He studied law and joined the New York bar. Stanford moved to California after the gold strike in 1848. He served as governor of the state during the Civil War. Stanford was elected to the U.S. Senate in 1885 and served until his death eight years later. In 1891, he founded the university that he named for his son, Leland Stanford Jr. near Palo Alto, California. Stanford died in 1893.

With the other members of the Big Four, Stanford incorporated the Central Pacific Railroad in 1861. The company built the western portion of the transcontinental railroad, completed in 1869. Stanford, as company president, served as the public face of the railroad. He and his associates acquired other transportation and water interests, creating a virtual transportation monopoly. They were dubbed the "Robber Barons" because of the wealth and power they wielded. Attempts to wrest power from these men were never entirely successful, and the Big Four remained an important force in California into the 20th century.

*National Archives*

# Biographies and Organizations
## A Question of Economics and Race, cont.

### CHINESE AMERICAN CITIZENS ALLIANCE

Ethnic support group founded by Chun Dick in 1895 in San Francisco, California. Originally called the "Native Sons of the Golden State in California," the organization was designed to confront anti-Chinese bigotry, to aid Chinese Americans in adapting to American culture, and to fight for civil rights. The group soon had chapters across the state. The leadership decided to go national: in 1915, the organization filed a new charter and changed its name to the Chinese American Citizens Alliance. The organization established a newspaper and fought several anti-immigration laws during the 20th century. It survives today, although rivaled by other groups such as the Chinese American Democratic Club.

### CHINESE CONSOLIDATED BENEVOLENT ASSOCIATION

An umbrella social service organization that provided informal representation to Chinese people in the United States primarily during the 19th century. The organization was popularly known as the Chinese Six Companies. It was more socially-focused than the Chinese Americans Citizens Alliance, helping new immigrants to find housing, medical care, and arranging shipment home for the deceased. But the group was politically active as well, protesting legislative and local discrimination. The organization was hampered by the restriction of new immigration following the passage of the Chinese Exclusion Act in 1882. Still, it endured into the 20th century, distributing government aid during the Depression and acting as an anti-communist force during the 1950s.

## IMMIGRATION RESTRICTION LEAGUE

Political action group founded by affluent Bostonians in 1894 who wanted to limit the rising numbers of immigrants coming to the United States. The group proposed instituting literacy tests to determine whether an immigrant would be admitted to the country. League members knew that many immigrants were poor and uneducated, so this would have established a very effective barrier to immigration. Congress introduced literacy tests for immigrants with the Immigration Act of 1917, and the League dissolved soon after. But its restrictive ideas are still visible in the Immigration Act of 1924, which limited immigration by national origin.

## WORKINGMEN'S PARTY OF CALIFORNIA

California grassroots political organization. In the 1870s, an economic depression gripped the eastern United States and many workers went to California to find employment. There they encountered influxes of Chinese immigrant laborers. The lack of jobs led to unrest, which grew more focused in 1877 when a general rail strike in the East set off waves of worker agitation. San Francisco's unemployed began organizing in empty sandlots around City Hall. The meetings led to riots in which Chinese businesses were burned. The mob also attempted to destroy the terminals of the steamship company that transported Chinese immigrants to California. In August 1877, a young Irish laborer named Dennis Kearney channeled this negative energy into a new labor party: the Workingmen's Party of California. Kearney spoke out against the state's wealthy railroadmen and the Chinese labor they hired, often advocating violence against both. The Party held a statewide convention in 1878. However, the party platform shifted away from racist denunciations of the Chinese and toward calls for the government to break up railroad monopolies and rein in the capitalists. In 1879, the Party carried most of the city offices in San Francisco and managed to get some blatantly anti-Chinese clauses inserted into the new state constitution. During the following year, the Party disintegrated because of infighting and the inexperience of its candidates.

# Phrases and Quotes
## A Question of Economics and Race

**"ETHNOLOGISTS DECLARE . . . THAT THE BRAIN CAPACITY LESS THAN 85 CUBIC INCHES IS UNFIT FOR FREE GOVERNMENT"**

Quotes such as this refer to a branch of 19th century thinking: scientific racism. It originated with the evolutionary theories of Darwin, applied to humans. In "social Darwinism," the races are believed to be unequal. "Survival of the fittest" causes some races to achieve and others to fail. Among Americans and Europeans, the white race was assumed to be at the top with all others ranked below. Looking for measurable data to validate these ideas, some scientists began examining the biological features of each race for the explanations of superiority and inferiority. Bodily measurements were linked to each race's intelligence and moral character. This quote is referring to skull measurements, saying that those of the Chinese indicated their "natural" inability to govern. Although it was based upon bad science and bigotry, scientific racism lingered into the 20th century. But when the Nazis adopted it to justify genocide, scientific racism was permanently discredited.

**"IDEA OF A CHINESE INVASION . . . "**

This quote is referring to hysterical fear among Americans of the 1880s that immigrants were about to pour into the country, overrunning it. To understand how this sentiment might arise, we must pair Chinese immigration on the West Coast with what was happening on the East Coast at the same time: 1880 to 1920 saw one of the heaviest waves of European immigration to America. The source of the immigration was southern and eastern Europe: Italians, Poles, Russians, Jews, and so on. These newcomers were people totally alien to established Americans. There was doubt about whether so many people, so different in appearance, language, and religion, could be assimilated into the American landscape. Americans on both coasts, confronted with alien ethnic groups, were feeling overwhelmed. It was feared that "traditional" American culture would change or be lost entirely.

## "THE MARTYRDOM OF ST. CRISPIN"

Crispin was a Catholic saint who supported himself as a shoemaker. He was beheaded and became a Christian martyr in the fourth century. Because of his profession, St. Crispin is the patron saint of shoemakers. When American shoe factory workers organized a labor union in 1867, they called it the Secret Order of the Knights of St. Crispin. It was the most powerful labor organization in the country at the time. In the summer of 1870, union workers at the Model Shoe Factory in North Adams, Massachusetts, went on strike. They were protesting low wages and the introduction of labor-saving machinery. To break the strike, the company owners imported seventy-five Chinese laborers from San Francisco (a move that was soon copied at other factories).

## "THE MONIED MEN, BACKED BY A REPUBLICAN PRESS AND PRESIDENT . . . "

This quote most likely refers to industrialists such as the "Big Four" of California, who imported Chinese immigrants for cheap manpower and for breaking strikes by labor unions. These men identified themselves with the Republican Party, which took a more permissive view of immigration than the Democrats. A perfect example is Republican President Chester A. Arthur, who strongly resisted signing the Chinese Exclusion Act into law, although he did so in the end. Republican journalists such as political cartoonist Thomas Nast and *New York Herald Tribune* editor Whitelaw Reid bolstered the Republican Party in print.

# Phrases and Quotes
## A Question of Economics and Race, cont.

### "THE PEOPLE ARE GOING TO HAVE TO BEGIN RISING UP AND USE ACTS OF VIOLENCE"

Anti-immigrant activists often successfully encouraged violence against Chinese laborers. Several examples stand out. The first was in Los Angeles on October 24, 1871. Two Chinese men in a fight accidentally killed a third man—a white. A mob stormed the city's Chinatown and shot, stabbed, or lynched nineteen Chinese men and boys. Another occurred at Rock Springs, Wyoming, in 1885. On September 2nd, a mob of white miners invaded the Chinese section of Rock Springs and opened fire on the population of about 600 people. By the time the violence ended, twenty-eight Chinese were dead. The following February in Seattle, violence erupted when an anti-Chinese group tried to deport most of the city's Chinese community by forcefully loading them onto a steamship. Anti-Chinese violence was reported in several other western states during the 1880s, including Colorado, Nevada, and Oregon.

### "SOCIETIES FOR MUTUAL AID AND ASSISTANCE"

Groups such as these—often called "fraternal" or "benevolent" aid societies—were very common in 19th-century America. Forerunners of modern labor unions, they often consisted of people of one profession or nationality banding together to pool resources and help each other in times of need.

### "THEY HAVE NO WIVES, CHILDREN, OR DEPENDENTS. THEY ARE IMPORTED BY COMPANIES . . . "

This quote refers to the fact that most 19th-century Chinese immigrants were males brought over to work. This was partly the result of Chinese custom. But in 1875, Congress passed the Page Law, which

expressly forbid unaccompanied Chinese women from entering the
United States. The law stated that this was to prevent a rise in prostitution rates. More likely, it was designed to keep the Chinese from
settling permanently in families or forming stable communities.

### "VIOLATE OUR TREATY OBLIGATIONS . . . "

This quote refers to a potential violation of the Burlingame Treaty
(1868). It was an agreement signed by China and the United States on
July 28, 1868 that established friendship, trade, and mutual rights of
immigration between the two nations. This treaty was one way that
America acknowledged the achievements of Chinese immigrants in the
building of the transcontinental railroad.

# Places and Things
## A Question of Economics and Race

*iStockPhoto.com*

### ANGEL ISLAND

Located in the middle of San Francisco Bay, Angel Island was used as an immigration inspection station for several decades. Between 1910 and 1940, about 175,000 Chinese were processed there. Some were confined—often for months and years at a time—in Angel Island's wooden barracks, where inspectors conducted grueling interrogations to determine whether the prospective Chinese immigrants were admissible. The facilities on Angel Island were gloomy. Most of the immigrants, young men in their teens, were deprived of education, recreation, and health care. Most of the immigration station on Angel Island was destroyed by fire in 1940.

### CENTRAL PACIFIC RAILROAD

Railroad founded by the "Big Four" in 1861. It built the western half of the transcontinental rail line, constructing track eastward from Sacramento, California, as the Union Pacific Railroad laid track west from Omaha, Nebraska. The two rail lines met at Promontory Summit, Utah, on May 10, 1869. The nation was finally knit together by a single transportation line that stretched from coast to coast.

The Union Pacific Railroad hired mainly Irish immigrants and Civil War veterans. But the Central Pacific hired thousands of Chinese immigrant laborers, even recruiting on farms in China.

### MAGNUSON ACT (1943)

This act repealed the Chinese Exclusion Act of 1882. The United States had entered World War I in 1941 after Japan attacked Pearl Harbor. Suddenly engaged in an Asian theater of war, the American government had to rethink its policies. China was also at war with the Japanese, which made that nation a natural ally. To facilitate friendship between the nations, the United States repealed its discriminatory Chinese immigration policies. Under the Act, Chinese residents already in the country also became eligible for citizenship.

# Events and Eras
## A Question of Economics and Race

### CULTURAL REVOLUTION

Period of intense political and social change in China instituted by leader Mao Zedong between 1966 and 1976. After the establishment of the People's Republic of China in 1949, Mao feared that capitalist influences were creeping into the new Communist state. To counteract this, he placed factories, universities, and whole cities under government control. The same was done with agricultural areas. The immediate result was chaos and economic stagnation. By the mid-1970s, China was under control of the military. An estimated two million people were killed during the Cultural Revolution, mainly educated and professional people.

### "GILDED AGE" AMERICA

Author Mark Twain used the term "Gilded Age" to describe the manners and customs of America's new wealthy class in the period of rapid industrialization and economic expansion following the end of the American Civil War. This period, which lasted through the 1880s, was characterized by gaudy lifestyles, unscrupulous business dealings, and widespread political corruption.

### IRISH IMMIGRATION

A very large number of Irish immigrants arrived in America during the late 1840s and 1850s. They were fleeing a terrible famine at home. Most Irish peasants lived on potatoes, and, in 1846, a fungal disease destroyed ninety percent or more of the potato crop. Years of starvation and disease followed; many took ships for America to escape. Although it slackened, Irish immigration continued for most of the 19th century. The arrival of a large number of Catholic, non-English speaking immigrants set off the first wave of anti-immigrant hysteria in American history.

# Background
## A Question of Economics and Race

### CHINESE AMERICANS IN THE LATE-19TH-CENTURY WEST

Chinese immigrants played a crucial role in the westward expansion of the United States, particularly in the building of the transcontinental railroad in the second half of the 19th century. Despite the fact that the Chinese filled an important labor need and proved to be extremely hard workers, white laborers resented their presence. Anti-Chinese riots took place in western cities such as Los Angeles, San Francisco, and Seattle. Bowing to heavy political pressure, the federal government stepped into the fray with the Chinese Exclusion Act of 1882, and the U.S. Supreme Court supported the government's stance in subsequent rulings.

The California gold rush of the mid-19th century led to a tremendous influx of people into California, and many of them were from China. California quickly became known as "Gum San" (Gold Mountain) in China, and by 1852, an estimated 25,000 Chinese had made it to Gold Mountain, although few of them struck it rich. Some decided to return home, but many remained behind and found employment as miners. They quickly earned reputations as hard workers who were willing to toil long hours for low pay. White miners resented the presence of these foreigners and did their best to drive them away. In 1852, the California legislature passed the Foreign Miner's Tax in an attempt to limit the number of Chinese and Mexican miners in the state.

The Chinese were forced to live in segregated communities. Many workers frustrated by the Foreign Miner's Tax became merchants in Chinatown or turned to domestic work such as cooking, gardening, or housekeeping to make a living. Discrimination against the Chinese continued throughout the 1850s and included such measures as denying them legal rights and excluding them from attending public schools. Still, the Chinese community thrived in San Francisco's Chinatown and built a Chinese theater and temple to make Chinese immigrants feel more at home. In addition, more and more Chinese were crossing the Pacific to America as the devastating Taiping Rebellion in China claimed millions of lives.

During the early 1860s, a massive project that would require thousands of hardened laborers was getting under way—the building of the transcontinental railroad. By 1865, the Central Pacific Railroad, later known as the Southern Pacific Railroad, had begun work in earnest on the western portion of the transcontinental railroad but was suffering from a labor shortage. The pay for working on the railroad was low, and white workers were deserting the railroad in droves for more lucrative opportunities in mining, particularly after new silver strikes were unearthed in nearby Nevada. Charles Crocker, the chief contractor for the Central Pacific, decided it was time to hire "coolies," a derogatory name for Chinese laborers. Despite their initial reluctance, company owners were soon impressed with the Chinese workers' performance. From the moment they began working on the transcontinental railroad, the Chinese performed well and willingly took on the most demanding and dangerous jobs.

Buoyed by their exceptional performance working on the transcontinental railroad, the stock of Chinese laborers went up in the late 1860s, culminating in the Burlingame Treaty, an agreement on friendship, trade, and mutual rights of immigration signed by China and the United States on July 28, 1868. Many more Chinese immigrants began to come to the West Coast of the United States and were now competing for jobs with railroad workers, many of whom found themselves unemployed after the golden spike ceremony signaled the completion of the transcontinental railroad in May, 1869. According to the 1870 U.S. census, 71,328 of the 550,247 people living in California at the time were Chinese. However, that same year, Congress deliberately denied Chinese the right to be naturalized as citizens because of their "undesirable qualities."

# Background
## A Question of Economics and Race, cont.

On the national level, Congress responded to the pressures from the growing anti-Asian movement by passing the Chinese Exclusion Act of 1882, which halted further immigration of Chinese into the United States for ten years. As discrimination and violence continued against the Chinese in America, some Chinese attempted to use the U.S. legal system to fight back. Near the end of the 1880s, the U.S. Supreme Court was faced with a challenge to the 1882 Chinese Exclusion Act. In the case of *Chae Chan Ping v. United States* (1889), the Court upheld the act, noting that Chinese laborers were aliens, not U.S. citizens. Three years later, the Geary Act of 1892 extended the Chinese Exclusion Act ban on immigration for another ten years, and it was extended again in 1902 before being extended indefinitely in 1904. It was finally repealed in 1943 during World War II, when China and the United States found themselves fighting together as allies against Japan.

# Sources

Choy, Philip, Lorraine Dong, and Marlon K. Horn, eds. *The Coming Man: 19th Century American Perceptions of the Chinese.* Seattle: University of Washington Press, 1994.

*Congressional Record.* Vol. 13. Washington, DC: Government Printing Office, 1882.

Foner, Philip and Daniel Rosenberg, eds., *Racism, Dissent, and Asian Americans from 1850 to the Present: A Documentary History.* Westport, CT: Greenwood Press, 1993.

Gyory, Andrew. *Closing the Gate: Race, Politics, and the Chinese Exclusion Act.* Chapel Hill: University of North Carolina Press, 1998.

Lee, Sharon M. "Asian Immigration and American Race Relations from Exclusion to Acceptance." *Ethnic and Racial Studies,* 1989, 12 (3): 369–390.

Lin, Han-Sheng. "Chinese Immigrants in the United States: Achievements and Problems." *Peace and Change,* 1975, 3(2/3): 52–67.

McClellan, Robert. *The Heathen Chinese: A Study of American Attitudes Toward the Chinese, 1890–1905.* Columbus: Ohio State University Press, 1971.

Miller, Stuart Creighton. "An East Coast Perspective to Chinese Exclusion, 1852–1882." *Historian,* 1971, 33 (2): 183–201.

Salyer, Lucy E. *Laws Harsh as Tigers: Chinese Immigrants and the Shaping of Modern Immigration Law.* Chapel Hill: University of North Carolina Press, 1995.

*San Francisco Chronicle.* 1 April 1882–18 May 1882.

*San Francisco Examiner.* 1 April 1882–18 May 1882.

Seager, Robert. "Some Denominational Reactions to Chinese Immigration to California, 1856–1892." *Pacific Historical Review,* 1959, 28 (1): 49–66.

Tsai, Shih-Shah Henry. *The Chinese Experience in America.* Bloomington: Indiana University Press, 1986.

# Acceptance with Conditions

# Defining Moment

Associated Press

Henry Romero/Reuters/Corbis

# Acceptance with Conditions

Established in 1942, the bracero program was a series of bilateral agreements between the Mexican and U.S. governments that allowed Mexican farm laborers to work temporarily in the southwestern United States. The program was designed to address U.S. labor shortages during World War II, when most U.S. workers were occupied in the war effort. From 1947 to 1949, more than 142,000 undocumented workers were legalized through the program. Although growers welcomed a source of cheap labor not organized by unions, the braceros themselves were subjected to low wages, no schooling for their children, and deplorable living conditions.

*Library of Congress*

*Mexican workers recruited and brought to the Arkansas valley, Colorado, Nebraska, and Minnesota by the Farm Security Administration (FSA) to harvest and process sugar beets under contract with the Inter-mountain Agricultural Improvement Association.*

During World War II, most American working men were conscripted into the armed services. Adding to the labor shortage in the West was the internment of thousands of Japanese and Japanese American farmers and agricultural workers. To increase the supply of available workers, the United States and Mexico agreed to implement the bracero measure, officially known as the Mexican Farm Labor Program. That action marked the birth of the temporary-worker program aimed at legalizing the migrant worker population.

Under the bracero program, Mexico allowed its workers to come to the United States for temporary renewable periods under regulated conditions. The program outlined a series of strict guidelines, including recruitment, a minimum wage, transportation, housing, and a savings program for the bracero's pay. Companies that violated the provisions were penalized by losing access to bracero labor. In addition, the U.S. government began investigating the substandard, abusive conditions to which the braceros were subjected, and in 1943, the U.S. Department of Labor began regulating those conditions. However, some braceros still endured inferior living conditions, excessive boarding charges, discrimination, and unnecessary wage deductions.

*The children of Mexican migrant workers pose under a sign at a Farm Security Administration camp. During the farm labor shortage of the 1940s, the U.S. government recruited Mexican laborers under the bracero program.*

*Library of Congress*

At the end of World War II, businesses involved in agriculture sought to continue the bracero program. Farmers and agribusinesses found that the steady stream of cheap labor was extremely profitable. Because no labor unions were involved in the employer-employee relationship, wages remained low. Perhaps for the same reason, farmers found the braceros to be a very manageable workforce. And since the program involved men who had left their families behind in Mexico, housing remained inexpensive. But despite the advantages it offered to American business, the bracero program did exact a social toll, mostly on the Mexican workers who participated. They were separated from their families for long periods of time and often lived in conditions that offered few comforts. Eventually, some workers refused to return home. Some rejected the bracero program altogether by refusing to sign new contracts. As a result, illegal immigration began to grow up alongside legal immigration, even though very large numbers of contracts were issued; half a million in 1956 alone.

# Acceptance with Conditions, cont.

The Immigration and Naturalization Service (INS) sought to address the growing illegal immigration problem, as did the U.S. Border Patrol, instituted in 1924. In 1954, as illegal immigration reached its peak, the agencies launched Operation Wetback ("wetback" being a derogatory term for illegal Mexican immigrants who swam the Rio Grande to reach the United States). During the Operation, 1.3 million undocumented Mexican workers were identified. Agents swept north from the border, rounding up illegal workers and deporting them to Mexico. However, in some cases legal workers and even U.S. citizens were mistakenly deported as a result of paperwork errors. Operation Wetback ended in 1957 after deporting 3.5 million Mexicans.

*Henry Romero/Reuters/Corbis*

*A former bracero holds up employment papers as he claims money collected by the United State's government on behalf of braceros was never distributed.*

The bracero program reached its zenith in the 1950s and gradually declined into the early 1960s. The program had been criticized for a long time, and eventually the critics helped to bring it to a close. Labor unions had been staunch opponents of the program for years because they said it kept down wages down and locked non-bracero workers out of the agricultural labor market. President John F. Kennedy took a critical look at the program in the early 1960s. In 1963, his administration decided to extend it for only one more year. They cited as a reason the problems of abuse within the system, including poor living conditions for the workers and depressed wages. The U.S. Congress terminated the bracero program in 1964.

## Lesson Overview

This activity introduces students to immigration issues of the 20th century, focusing upon the details of the Mexican bracero experience. Students will need some background on the early days of World War II and the role played by the U.S. and Mexico in the conflict. The activity is divided into three parts.

In Part I, the students will read portions of the bracero agreement between the U.S. and Mexico (1943) and discuss what motives might underlie the document on both sides.

In Part II, the students will read quotes from a bracero narrative and view photos that illustrate the bracero story. They will create a single narrative presentation from the material.

In Part III, the students will assume the role of a bracero, complete with ID card, and read two contrasting views of the bracero experience. Then they will bring all of the various viewpoints they have experienced to a short creative writing assignment.

# Acceptance with Conditions

## Authors

**CHRIS MULLIN**
SANTA YNEZ VALLEY
UNION HIGH SCHOOL

**BRETT PIERSMA**
SANTA YNEZ VALLEY
UNION HIGH SCHOOL

# Lesson Plan Part I
## Class Discussion

To begin this activity, the teacher will write the following question on the front board or project it from a data projector: *What do you think are primary motivating factors that compel people to leave their homelands for another country?* Students quick-write for several minutes on the question and then the teacher solicits their answers. On the board, the teacher writes "Push Factors" and "Pull Factors" in separate columns and explains each category (as described by Professor LeMay in the Introduction). As students share their answers, the teacher writes them in the appropriate categories (for example, "civil war" would be placed under "Push Factors" whereas "job opportunities" might be placed under "Pull Factors").

The teacher should then explain that students will be learning about a critical era in United States and Mexican history in addition to learning general themes about immigration. The teacher passes out a photocopy of Excerpts 2 through 7 to six different students. The teacher explains to students that as a class they will be reading excerpts from the 1943 bracero agreement and will put each document in a category as bene-fiting American farmers, braceros, or both. Below their quick-write, students should draw three columns as follows:

| Benefits Farm Owners | Benefits Braceros | Benefits Both |
|---|---|---|
|  |  |  |

The teacher should begin by reading Excerpt 1 to the class. Then, students read Excerpts 2 through 7 in order out loud to the class and allow students time to choose which column that particular portion of the agreement fits into.

The teacher uses the following questions to debrief this portion of the activity through a class discussion:

- Why do you think the United States was suffering from a labor shortage in 1943?
- Why do you think the agreement contained certain protections for the braceros?
- Overall, who benefits the most from this program, the United States or the braceros?

# Lesson Plan Part II
## The "Tea Party"

For the second part of this activity, the teacher should explain to the students that the class will collectively tell the story of the life of a real bracero by assembling a montage of images and quotes.

The teacher should photocopy Quotes 1–15 and Photos 1–15 and distribute them to the students (half will have Quotes and half will have Photos). Each student should receive a copy of Map 1 so that he or she can appreciate the length of the bracero's journey. The teacher should also make and keep a copy of Activity Sheet 1 so that he or she can follow and maintain the order of the Quotes.

Once all the students have either a quote or an image, the teacher explains that the students should now "tea party" with other members of the class for at least ten minutes. During this time, students walk around the room and read their quotes to other students or show other students their pictures. Every student should view and discuss all of the Photos and Quotes.

The teacher explains that by the end of the tea party, everyone with a quote should pair up with someone whose picture seems to reflect that portion of the bracero's story and prepare to present the class montage.

For the presentation, students arrange themselves around the room in pairs, in order by Quote number (1–15). Students read aloud each Quote in order while their partners hold up the pictures for the class to see.

For this portion, the teacher may want to prepare a slideshow ahead of time with the quotes and images to go along with the storytelling.

## Activity
LESSON PLAN PART II

For this portion of the activity, you will need copies of:

ACTIVITY SHEETS
• Activity Sheet 1, p. 86

Students will need copies of:

PRIMARY SOURCES
• Map 1, p. 102
• Quotes 1–15, pp. 94–101
• Photos 1–15, pp. 103–117

# Activity Sheet 1
## Reading Order for Bracero Story

#1 "I was born . . . "

#2 "I was a bracero . . . "

#3 "We had four . . . "

#4 "Instead of . . . "

#5 "We got on . . . "

#6 "Once we . . . "

#7 "Then they'd send . . . "

#8 "We were hired . . . "

#9 "I went to Santa Maria . . . "

#10 "I think at that . . . "

#11 "We slept in big . . . "

#12 "We could . . . "

#13 "The foremen . . . "

#14 "When the farm workers' . . . "

#15 "It was the . . . "

# Lesson Plan Part III
## Becoming a Bracero

For the final part of the activity, the teacher should explain to the students that they will be required to carry identification cards with them everywhere they go much the same way braceros were required to. Photocopy the sample identification cards and give one to each student.

The teacher should instruct students to personalize the cards at home with a picture and relevant personal information and bring it back to class the next day.

The teacher should check students' cards every day when they enter the class and even during breaks and lunch. The teacher might want to incorporate a point system whereby students are graded down each time they are caught without a card.

After several days of requiring students to carry their identification cards, the teacher should then pass out copies of Document 1 and Document 2, which are copies of the narrative "My Impressions" by Enrique Parra Ramirez and the poem "Illusion" by H. Uribe Gonzalez.

These writings are read as a class and their meanings are discussed. Finally, students should write their own two-stanza poems based on all they have heard, seen, read, and experienced through these activities. The poem can be in first person or from whatever viewpoint they prefer.

## Activity
### LESSON PLAN PART III

For this portion of the activity, students will need copies of:

ACTIVITY SHEETS
• Activity Sheet 2, p. 88 (cut into individual placards, one card per student)

PRIMARY SOURCES
• Document 1, p. 118
• Document 2, p. 119

# Activity Sheet 2
## Becoming a Bracero, cont.

---

**SAMPLE**
**ALIEN LABORER'S PERMIT**

Name: _____
Home address: _____
Date of birth: _____
Place of birth: _____
Admitted at: _____

L x~~133449800~~ 3464086

*Firma de Portador*

Contracted to: _____
For employment as agricultural worker under P.L. 78 in (Area): _____
Admitted to: _____

*(Signature of Admitting Officer)*

1-100 C    **IMMIGRATION ACTIVITY** - Immigration and Naturalization Service

---

**SAMPLE**
**ALIEN LABORER'S PERMIT**

Name: _____
Home address: _____
Date of birth: _____
Place of birth: _____
Admitted at: _____

L x~~133449800~~ 3464086

*Firma de Portador*

Contracted to: _____
For employment as agricultural worker under P.L. 78 in (Area): _____
Admitted to: _____

*(Signature of Admitting Officer)*

1-100 C    **IMMIGRATION ACTIVITY** - Immigration and Naturalization Service

*ABC-CLIO*

Bracero ID cards.

# Primary Sources

Acceptance with
Conditions

# Excerpts
## from Bracero Agreement of 1943

**EXCERPT 1**

[A letter from the American ambassador to the Mexican Minister of Foreign Affairs]

Embassy of the United States of America
Mexico, D.F., April 26, 1943.

No. 1214

Excellency:

I have the honor to refer to the note No. 317 dated April 26, 1943 in which Your Excellency formulates certain proposals made by the Mexican Government for making the Agreement of August 4, 1942 between the governments of the United States of America and Mexico a more workable instrument under which Mexican agricultural workers may be recruited in Mexico to work in the United States for a temporary period.

The United States representatives who have been discussing the proposed changes with the representatives designated by the Mexican Government for this purpose have been gratified by the generous spirit of cooperation which has animated these discussions and which has helped to bring them to a successful conclusion.

I am incorporating into this note the text of the Agreement of August 4, 1942 and indicating by underlining those additions or changes agreed upon by my Government:

# Excerpts
## from Bracero Agreement of 1943, cont.

**EXCERPT 2**

General Provisions

1) It is understood that Mexicans contracting to work in the United

   States shall not be engaged in any military service.

**EXCERPT 3**

2) Mexicans entering the United States as a result of this

   understanding shall not suffer discriminatory acts of any kind

   in accordance with the Executive Order No. 8802 issued at the

   White House June 25, 1941.

# Excerpts
## from Bracero Agreement of 1943, cont.

**EXCERPT 4**

Wages and Employment

a. (1) Wages to be paid the worker shall be the same as those paid
for similar work to other agricultural laborers under the same
conditions within the same area, in the respective regions of desti-
nation. Piece rates shall so be set as to enable the worker of
average ability to earn the prevailing wage. In any case wages for
piece work or hourly work will not be less than 30 cents per hour.

**EXCERPT 5**

a. (2) On the basis of prior authorization from the Mexican
Government salaries lower than those established in the previous
clause may be paid those emigrants admitted into the United
States as members of the family of the worker under contract and
who, when they are in the field, are able also to become agricultural laborers but who, by their condition of age or sex, cannot
carry out the average amount of ordinary work.

# Excerpts
## from Bracero Agreement of 1943, cont.

PRIMARY
SOURCES
DOCUMENT

### EXCERPT 6

b. The worker shall be exclusively employed as an agricultural laborer for which he has been engaged; any change from such type of employment or any change of locality shall be made with the express approval of the worker and with the authority of the Mexican Government.

PRIMARY
SOURCES
DOCUMENT

### EXCERPT 7

d. Work of minors under 14 years shall be strictly prohibited, and they shall have the same schooling opportunities as those enjoyed by children of other agricultural laborers.

# Quotes
## from "The Story of a Bracero"
## by Rigoberto Garcia Perez

**QUOTE 1**

I was born in Lalgodona, Michoacan, January 26, 1934. My father owned some land, but he had to keep selling it off, and in the end, he lost all of it. He became a bracero when the war started with Germany. They always made good money, the bracero. He rebuilt his house and tried to recover his land, but he couldn't.

**QUOTE 2**

I was a bracero from '56 to '59. I was in Watsonville six months before I got married. My wife and I would write each other, and I'd ask her to wait for me until I returned. She didn't like my leaving, but she stuck with me. I told her, 'I'll just go this once, and I'll be back in time to do the planting.' I went off to work, but always with the idea I'd come back and we'd use the money to do more on our farm.

# Quotes
## from "The Story of a Bracero," cont.

**QUOTE 3**

We had four hectares of onions in Mexico, but the price fell, and the crop just stayed in the ground. So I said, Well, I better go to the United States as a bracero. The next year, when I came back to Mexico, we had a good crop of camote. We put our backs into it, and irrigated, and we had no competition. We were the lords of the market. But afterwards, I thought again, Well, I better go back to the United States.

**QUOTE 4**

Instead of hopping freights and all that, we could go a different way. I went to the contracting station in Sonora, in Empalme. It was very easy to get work. There were people there who would sign you up, for $300 a month at that time. They'd get a thousand or two thousand people a day.

# Quotes
## from "The Story of a Bracero," cont.

**QUOTE 5**

We got on the train and went all the way to Mexicali, where we got

on buses to the border. From there, they took us to El Centro.

Thousands of men came every day.

**QUOTE 6**

Once we got there, they'd send us in groups of two hundred, as

naked as we came into the world, into a big room, about sixty feet

square. Then men would come in in masks, with tanks on their backs,

and they'd fumigate us from top to bottom. Supposedly we were

flea-ridden, germ-ridden. No matter, they just did it.

# Quotes
## from "The Story of a Bracero," cont.

**QUOTE 7**

Then they'd send us into a huge bunkhouse, where the contractors would come from the growers associations in counties like San Joaquin County, Yolo, Sacramento, Fresno and so on. The heads of the associations would line us up. When they saw someone they didn't like, they'd say, 'You, no.' Others, they'd say, 'You, stay.' Usually, they didn't want people who were old—just young people. Strong ones, right? And I was young, so I never had problems getting chosen.

PRIMARY
SOURCES
DOCUMENT

**QUOTE 8**

We were hired in El Centro and given our contracts, usually for 45 days. It was an agreement from one government to the other. The contract had to have the signature of the mayor of your town, guaranteeing your reputation. You also had to have experience picking in Mexico. When your contract was over, they'd put you on a bus back to El Centro. And there they'd give you the passage back to Empalme.

# Quotes
from "The Story of a Bracero," cont.

**QUOTE 9**

I went to Santa Maria, where we picked strawberries. From there they renewed our contracts and sent us to Suisun, and we picked pears there. When we were through, the rancher said, 'Now we're going to Davis.' And from there they sent us back to Mexico.

**QUOTE 10**

I think at that time our wage was 80¢ an hour. In the tomatoes it was piecework—20¢ a box. That was pretty good if you could pick a hundred boxes. But the work was a killer, really hard. They'd give you two rows, which could give you 50 boxes, and you could do that in half a day.

**QUOTE 11**

We slept in big bunkhouses. It was like being in the army. Each person had their own bed, one on top of the other, with a mattress, blanket and so on. They'd tell us to keep the place clean, to make our beds when we got up. We woke up when they sounded a horn or turned on the lights. We'd make our beds and go to the bathroom, eat breakfast, and they'd give us our lunch—some tacos or a couple of sandwiches, an apple, and a soda. When we got back to camp, we'd wash up before we went to eat.

**QUOTE 12**

We could leave the camp if we wanted to go into town. In Stockton there was a Spaniard who had a drugstore and a radio station. He would send buses out to the camps to give people a ride. He was making a business out of selling us shirts, clothes, and medicine.

# Quotes
## from "The Story of a Bracero," cont.

PRIMARY
SOURCES
DOCUMENT

**QUOTE 13**

The foremen really abused people. A lot was always expected of you, and they always demanded even more. There were places where braceros went out on strike, or stopped work. One of my brothers went on strike in Phoenix because they were picking cotton and the crop was bad.

PRIMARY
SOURCES
DOCUMENT

**QUOTE 14**

When the farm workers' movement came along, we already knew about organizing and strikes from people who'd participated in those movements. My father had been on strike in Mexico, too. He'd tell me that when the boss doesn't understand you have to hit him where it hurt, in his pocketbook. If you don't, he won't see you. Like Cesar Chavez said, you have to educate both—the exploiter and the exploited. If you don't educate both sides, you can't have a future.

# Quotes
## from "The Story of a Bracero," cont.

**QUOTE 15**

It was the beginning of the life I'm leading now. Thanks to those experiences, we survived, and here I am. I have two countries, just me, one person. I can cross the border, and live in my own land, and I can live happily in this country, too. I came as an alambrista, and then back came as a bracero. Eventually I got my papers and lived like any other person. But I always remembered how I got here. Illegal [sic], a bracero.

# Map 1

UNITED STATES

**MEXICO**

*Gulf of Mexico*

*PACIFIC OCEAN*

Michoacan

0         900 mi

0       900 km

*ABC-CLIO*

Map of Mexico.

# Photo 1

*Howard R. Rosenberg, "Snapshots in a Farm Labor Tradition," Labor Management Decisions, Winter–Spring, 1993*

After the contract is explained to them, the braceros return to sign the agreement, which is returned to them in quadruplicate.

# Photo 2

*Associated Press*

A bracero harvests
chili peppers on a
United States farm.

# Photo 3

*Howard R. Rosenberg, "Snapshots in a Farm Labor Tradition," Labor Management Decisions, Winter–Spring, 1993*

Braceros sign up at a
stadium in Mexico to
obtain temporary work in
the United States.

# Photo 4

*Howard R. Rosenberg, "Snapshots in a Farm Labor Tradition," Labor Management Decisions, Winter–Spring, 1993*

After the men have been given a physical examination and x-rays, they are lined up in groups in the seating section of the stadium so that the contract, paragraph by paragraph, can be explained to them in Spanish.

# Photo 5

*Howard R. Rosenberg, "Snapshots in a Farm Labor Tradition," Labor Management Decisions, Winter–Spring, 1993*

Braceros receive smallpox
vaccinations as part of the
registration process.

# Photo 6

*Howard R. Rosenberg, "Snapshots in a Farm Labor Tradition," Labor Management Decisions, Winter–Spring, 1993*

Braceros line up for x-rays
as part of registration
requirements.

# Photo 7

*Howard R. Rosenberg, "Snapshots in a Farm Labor Tradition," Labor Management Decisions, Winter–Spring, 1993*

Bracero fingerprints are

processed.

# Photo 8

Reyes Barron Ayres, of Rancho La Noria, Huimilpan, Mexico, is shown picking strawberries on a farm in Alameda County, California, in June 1963.

*Associated Press*

# Photo 9

*Associated Press*

A Mexican migratory laborer, employed under the bracero program, harvests tomatoes in Southern California.

# Photo 10

*Howard R. Rosenberg, "Snapshots in a Farm Labor Tradition," Labor Management Decisions, Winter–Spring, 1993*

New braceros receive

registration packets.

# Photo 11

*Associated Press, University of Texas El Paso Library*

This 1950s photo shows
braceros leaving
Chihuahua City, Mexico,
for El Paso, Texas.

# Photo 12

*Howard R. Rosenberg, "Snapshots in a Farm Labor Tradition," Labor Management Decisions, Winter–Spring, 1993*

New braceros receive a
contract overview as they
gather in stadium seating.

# Photo 13

*Associated Press*

A border patrol inspector checks a bracero's identification card.

# Photo 14

*Associated Press*

A former bracero reflects on his experiences as a temporary worker in the United States.

# Photo 15

*Leonard Nadel/National Museum of American History/Reuters/Corbis*

Braceros cross the
border in 1956.

# Document 1
## "My Impressions" by Enrique Parra Ramirez

I feel so very happy to have come here to work on the railway lines of North America. I am happy not only because I have come to know this Great Land of Marvels but also because I have come to meet my obligations as a good Mexican citizen and to collaborate and help attain a victory for peace. I do this not as a soldier on the battlefields but rather as a worker on the work fields. While my countrymen fought on the frontlines, my fellow workers and I cooperate by working the railroads and others work in agriculture as well in order to assist this benevolent country the United States. We fulfill our commitment with our dear homeland showing in this fashion affection and friendship as good allies. We show that we know how to reciprocate the friendship that all of the United Nations has shown us.

# Document 2
## "Illusion" by H. Uribe Gonzalez

What is it that you seek, poor pilgrim

that you leave your home and homeland with pressured step

Walking without direction or judgment

In light and shadows and on thorny paths?


I dream of relieving my outcast condition

Strengthen my spirit and soul

I am confident that I will find all of these things

Asking Him to help and guide me.


Why do you insist on useless wandering?

Longing to find all this in foreign lands?

Return to your homeland, oh poor pilgrim

Be happy in your home, do not dream of quarrels.

# Glossary Words, Ideas, or Movements
## Acceptance with Conditions

**ALAMBRISTA** Spanish term for illegal Mexican immigrant crossing into the United States; literal translation is "tightrope walker."

**BURGESS** An officer or an elite citizen of a town or borough; member of the ruling class in a locality.

**CAMOTE** Spanish term for a tropical variety of sweet potato.

**CONTRACTING STATIONS** Mexican men wanting to participate in the bracero program traveled—sometimes great distances—to prearranged points within Mexico for screening and recruitment, which were in several cities over the years. One of these was in Sonora in the northern state of Empalme, others were in Mexico City, Hidalgo, Ciudad Juarez, Guadalajara, Irapuato, and Monterrey. Once at the recruiting station, the prospective workers waited in long lines. The workers were interviewed by U.S. immigration and United States Employment Service (USES) officials. The workers had to prove that they were experienced farm workers because urbanites were excluded from the bracero program. This they did by showing officials the calluses on their hands. Once accepted, the men were fingerprinted and issued identification cards.

**OPERATION WETBACK OF 1954** A short-term program for rounding up and deporting illegal Mexican immigrants begun by the Immigration and Naturalization Service (INS) in Texas. The U.S. government perceived the need for such an effort because of the system breakdowns and corruption that plagued the bracero program. Illegal workers were crossing the borders even during the height of the program. Many were willing to work for less than the braceros, and Americans bribed Mexican officials to let them through. In the 1950s, illegal immigration increased sixty-fold. In July 1954, the INS began rounding up and deporting thousands of illegal Mexican workers and their American-born children (who were American citizens). Complaints in the United States and Mexico brought the program to an end, but not before the INS claimed it had sent 1.3 million undocumented workers back to Mexico.

**PILGRIM** A person journeying to find something; frequently associated with searching for religious sites or holy experiences.

**PROLETARIAT** The working classes; a term often used in Marxist teachings.

# Biographies and Organizations
Acceptance with Conditions

### CAMACHO, MANUEL ÁVILA

President of Mexico (1940–1946). Camacho was born in the state of Puebla in 1897. He joined the military, rising to the rank of general. He was appointed secretary of national defense in 1937. As a politician, Camacho was a moderate, seeking to reconcile factions within his country on issues such as the Catholic Church and land reform. Camacho died in 1955.

Ávila Camacho was president of Mexico during all of World War II. He supported the Allies from the earliest days of the war, but the rest of his nation remained neutral until the Germans sank two Mexican oil tankers in 1942. This act led to a declaration of war against Germany and Japan. Mexico became the second of two southern American nations that sent troops into World War II (the first was Brazil). Camacho was willing to work closely with the United States in the war effort. The two nations collaborated on hemisphere defense, trade agreements, and labor exchange (most notably, the bracero program) The closeness and interdependence of this wartime relationship would be carried into future decades.

*Corbis*

### CHAVEZ, CESAR

Organizer of successful migrant workers' union in California in the 1960s and 1970s. Chavez was born in Yuma, Arizona, in 1927. His parents were Mexican migrant farm workers, and Chavez received little formal education, dropping out of school to work the fields. He served in the navy during World War II. After the war, he organized and aided fellow farm workers, dissatisfied with the approach taken by other aid groups. Chavez died in 1993.

In 1962, Chavez formed a grassroots labor movement for Mexican migrant workers—the National Farm Workers Association (NWFA)—when he saw that community activists were not reaching the people.

This group merged with other agricultural unions to become the United Farm Workers of America (UFW) in 1967. The UFW received considerable support from the American Civil Rights Movement that was in full swing at the time. Through such support and the help of other unions, UFW workers were able to maintain a strike against California grape growers that lasted for five years. Eventually, the growers gave in and negotiated a contract. This was the first in a series of victories in which agribusiness was brought to the negotiating table and conditions were improved for agricultural laborers in America.

## KENNEDY, JOHN F.

P resident of the United States (1961–1963). John F. Kennedy was born in Brookline, Massachusetts, in 1917. He graduated from Harvard in 1940 and fought in the Pacific during World War II. He served in the House and Senate in the 1950s, before winning the Democratic nomination for the presidency in 1960. He won the election by a slim margin. After entangling the United States in the Bay of Pigs invasion of Cuba, presiding over the opening days of the Civil Rights Movement, and guiding the nation through the Cuban Missile Crisis, Kennedy was assassinated in November, 1963.

Before he was elected president, John F. Kennedy wrote a book entitled *A Nation of Immigrants* that applauded the important contributions of immigrants to American development. Once president, Kennedy requested that Congress repeal the restrictive Immigration Act of 1924. He was assassinated before this could be done, but the 1924 legislation was replaced by more liberal immigration policies in 1965.

# Biographies and Organizations
## Acceptance with Conditions, cont.

Kennedy also reached out to the nations of the Western Hemisphere with the "Alliance for Progress," an initiative for cooperation with Latin America and a pledge of U.S. aid for economic development in the region. The Kennedy administration believed that ending the bracero program fit in very well with this plan. The braceros were being treated poorly, being underpaid, and living in appalling conditions. Prominent Hispanic figures such as Cesar Chavez, wishing to improve conditions for Mexican workers, also believed that the bracero program was doing more harm than good. American labor unions pointed out that they could not organize American labor with an infinite supply of cheaper workers undercutting their bargaining power. As a result of Kennedy's goals and outside pressures, the bracero program was dismantled.

*Library of Congress*

### ROOSEVELT, FRANKLIN D.

President of the United States (1933–1945). Franklin D. Roosevelt was born in Hyde Park, New York, in 1882 to an upper-class family. He attended Harvard and Columbia Law School. Roosevelt married a distant cousin, Eleanor Roosevelt (niece of former president Theodore Roosevelt), in 1905. Roosevelt was elected governor of New York, where he gained a reputation as a compassionate reformer as the Great Depression took hold of the nation. This aspect of his political persona earned him the Democratic nomination for president in 1932. He was elected in a landslide after promising the suffering nation a "New Deal": recover, relief, and reform. After being reelected four times, guiding the nation through the Great Depression, and seeing World War II through into its last days, Roosevelt died in 1945.

Because of his experiences in the Great Depression, Franklin Roosevelt was keenly aware of the labor situation in America. When he took office, nearly twenty-five percent of Americans were unemployed. His administration established massive programs such as the Works Progress Administration (WPA) to create jobs. It established the National Labor Relations Board (NLRB) to oversee union activities and protect the workers' right to organize. When World War II began, he considered it partly as a labor problem. In his Labor Day address of 1941, Roosevelt laid out his vision of America as "the arsenal of democracy." He called upon American business to produce the goods and munitions that would bring down the Axis powers. Roosevelt saw the war as one of industrial production as well as strategy: an area dependent on the size of the labor force and acceptable employer-worker relationships. When the United States entered the war in 1941, military production went into high gear. Very soon, the nation was in need of more labor, and the Roosevelt administration set out to get it. American representatives in Mexico City approached the Mexican government about a guest-worker program that would import Mexican workers to take over agricultural jobs, freeing Americans for war industries and the military. American need happened to coincide with a low point in the Mexican agricultural economy: Mexico had many unemployed farm workers who were happy to go to the United States. The needs of both nations meshed well and contributed to their strong working relationship during the war.

## UNITED FARM WORKERS OF AMERICA (UFW)

L abor union of mainly Mexican agricultural workers in the United States, organized by Cesar Chavez in the early 1960s. The union began as a grassroots California organization devoted to securing better working conditions for agricultural laborers using consumer boycotts and negotiation. At this time, agricultural workers were not recognized by the National Labor Relations Board (NLRB), which oversaw conditions in other industries. The UFW had a significant affect on the grape, lettuce, and strawberry farmers of California and citrus growers in Florida. It negotiated successfully with employers for three-year work contracts with higher wages, health benefits, and a pledge to hire unionized workers. However, infighting with other unions and employers led to strike violence in 1973 in which three people were killed and sixty more wounded. The governor of California was forced to step in to stop the chaos, installing the Agricultural Labor Relations Board to regulate union activities.

# Court Cases, Amendments, and Acts
## Acceptance with Conditions

### EXECUTIVE ORDER 8802 (1941)

An important piece of civil rights legislation, often called the "Second Emancipation Proclamation." America on the eve of World War II was racially segregated. African Americans in particular faced social, economic, and legislative discrimination. Realizing that America needed to mobilize its entire workforce to win the war, and prompted by civil rights leaders, President Franklin Roosevelt issued an executive order forbidding discrimination against workers of any race by companies contracted to produce materials for the federal government. When the bracero program was introduced in 1943, the rights of Mexican guest workers were protected by the order, which remained in effect until superseded by the Civil Rights Act of 1964.

### IMMIGRATION ACT OF 1965

This act replaced the Immigration Act of 1924 and removed most quotas by national origin. The 1965 act replaced nationality quotas with a "rankings list" that gave priority to the children and spouses of legal immigrants, skilled workers, and the siblings of citizens.

Although the 1965 Act loosened immigration considerably, it had the opposite effect on *legal* Mexican immigration. Western Hemisphere nations had been excluded from the 1924 quotas. As one of these nations, Mexico had not been held to a quota. Unlimited immigration access and the bracero program had combined to create a back-and-forth migration pattern for many workers that lasted for decades. However, the 1965 act imposed a quota of 120,000 immigrants per year for all of the Americas. A 1976 amendment tightened the provisions further by restricting each Western Hemisphere nation to a maximum of 20,000 immigrants per year, Mexico included. However, this cap was nowhere near the actual numbers of Mexicans entering the country. The result was a huge increase in the numbers of illegal immigrants flowing into the United States.

# Phrases and Quotes
## Acceptance with Conditions

### "AGREEMENT OF AUGUST 4, 1942"

Refers to Mexican-American treaty that established the Mexican Farm Labor Program, known familiarly as the "bracero program." That action marked the birth of the temporary-worker program aimed at legalizing and regularizing the migrant worker population. Under the bracero program, Mexico allowed its workers to come to the United States for temporary renewable periods under regulated conditions. The bracero program specifically outlined a series of guidelines, including recruitment, a minimum wage, transportation, housing, and a savings program. Initially, braceros were limited to agricultural work, but in 1943, their role was extended to include American railroads.

### "ALWAYS WITH THE IDEA I'D COME BACK AND WE'D USE THE MONEY TO DO MORE ON OUR FARM"

This bracero is describing a common pattern among Mexicans immigrating to the United States over the years. It is called "circular migration." Under this system, workers came to the United States to work for short periods, returned to Mexico with their wages, and came back to repeat the process. The close proximity of the United States and Mexico, the cyclical nature of agricultural work, and the higher rates of pay in the United States made this a practical economic arrangement. The bracero program helped to increase the popularity of this type of immigration. It is still common.

### "GENEROUS SPIRIT OF COOPERATION . . . "

Mexico and the United States worked closely together as allies during World War II. Mexican president Manuel Ávila Camacho and American President Franklin D. Roosevelt agreed to several joint strategic endeavors, including the bracero program. By allowing foreign workers to take over agricultural and railroad jobs, America was able to maintain vital home front operations while sending large numbers of men to fight a two-front war.

# Phrases and Quotes
## Acceptance with Conditions, cont.

### "I HAVE TWO COUNTRIES, JUST ME, ONE PERSON"

The ease of traveling back and forth between the United States and Mexico under the bracero program, added to America's eagerness to hire this labor because of shortages, seems to have made this bracero feel at home in both countries.

### "IT WAS LIKE BEING IN THE ARMY"

Life for many braceros appears to have resembled military life: regimented activities and physical examinations were part of the deal. Living conditions for the bracero workers in the United States varied, but they appear to have been kept to the basic necessities. Often accommodations consisted of military-like barracks made from tents or old barns, with rows of bunks in which large numbers of workers were crowded together. By the time Cesar Chavez and the United Farm Workers (UFW) began protesting the treatment of Mexican migrant workers in the 1960s, conditions had deteriorated even further, with even the bare minimums of hygiene neglected.

### "PLACES WHERE BRACEROS WENT OUT ON STRIKE, OR STOPPED WORK"

The bracero program did not always operate smoothly and often suffered from gross abuses. The very first braceros to arrive in California went on strike immediately: the pay was not what they had been promised. In this case, the farmers raised the wages. At the other end of the spectrum, braceros were sometimes used to break strikes held by American workers. This behavior was expressly forbidden by the bracero agreements. It also left the guest workers vulnerable to attack on every side. By February 1943, instances of ill-treatment had filtered back to Mexico. The Mexican government suspended the program, only allowing it to go forward again when the U.S. government promised to improve conditions and monitor the situation more closely. But abuses continued. Idaho passed laws that forced braceros to remain at their jobs, or they would be arrested. While awaiting deportation, they would be forced to work without pay. In many cases, the only power of protest in the hands of the workers was the refusal to work.

## "THEY ALWAYS MADE GOOD MONEY, THE BRACERO"

The agricultural economy in Mexico had been depressed for decades
when the bracero program was instituted in 1943. Pay was traditionally
lower there than in the United States: at the close of the 19th century,
a Mexican farm worker had 1/14th the purchasing power of an
American in a comparable job (Miller and Miller, 1996). In addition, a
million peasants or more had been killed in the Mexican Revolution of
1910. With fewer people to work the land, farm yields had dropped
dramatically. Surviving workers found themselves with less and less
work. They responded eagerly to calls from the United States to come
work the farms. Although there were complaints about wages and
strikes, many braceros preferred working in the United States to the
alternative of attempting to find work at home.

## "TO COLLABORATE AND HELP ATTAIN A VICTORY FOR PEACE. I DO THIS NOT AS A SOLDIER ON THE BATTLEFIELDS BUT RATHER AS A WORKER ON THE WORK FIELDS . . . "

Mexico entered World War II in May, 1942 after the Germans sank two
Mexican oil tankers. This unprovoked attack was not unlike the Pearl
Harbor bombing that drew America into the war in 1941: comparable
events encouraged fellow feeling between the neighboring countries.
The two nations would work together throughout the war. This bracero
found working in the United States to be a patriotic duty. In helping
America to keep her home front functioning, he was contributing to the
joint U.S.–Mexican effort to defeat the Axis powers. In the early days of
the bracero program, then, there was a spirit of equal striving toward a
common goal on both sides. Economy, cooperation, and patriotism
were intertwined.

# Background
## Acceptance with Conditions

### A HISTORY OF U.S.–MEXICAN IMMIGRATION

From its earliest occurrences in the 1890s to the most current wave, economic interdependence has been threaded through Mexican immigration. In a famous speech, Mexican president Porfirio Diaz, who presided from 1876 to 1911, lamented that Mexico is "so far from God and so near the United States." He pinned his hopes for economic growth on the country's northern neighbor, the United States. Hoping to spur an anemic Mexican economy, Diaz promptly encouraged foreign investment while decimating indigenous and *mestizo* (people of mixed European and Indian parentage) rural communities.

The United States became Mexico's primary foreign investor, pumping millions of dollars into the economy. As a small cadre of Mexican industrialists fell in with U.S. corporate magnates, indigenous and mestizo peasants were dispossessed of land. Newfound land policies promoting industrialism eroded traditional communal subsistence farming, a mainstay of indigenous communities. An expansive turn-of-the-twentieth-century population boom and a rising cost of living spurred the first wave of Mexican immigrants.

While those cataclysmic changes occurred in Mexico, the United States likewise experienced a second Industrial Revolution, which occurred in railroad, mining, and agriculture in the Southwest. Mining, one of the first industries to employ Mexican laborers, conveniently pulled immigrants across the invisible dividing line. In northern Mexico, mining, affected by foreign investors, developed quickly. By the 1890s, such southwestern mining towns as Clifton and Morenci, Arizona, had benefited from the arrival of Mexican peasants. Transportation provided another major employer, as approximately 35,000 to 50,000 Mexicans assisted in the completion of the Southern Pacific and Santa Fe railways. However, the advent of agricultural business provided the bulk of the jobs. At the same time, restrictive immigration acts that stemmed the arrival of Asian and European immigrants allowed the flow of Mexican immigration to continue virtually unchecked.

Meanwhile, the Mexican Revolution of 1910 catapulted hundreds of thousands of Mexican nationals to the United States. The revolution, which resulted in the deaths of nearly one million Mexicans, broadened the scope of immigration. Middle-class Mexican businessmen, along with political activists and working-class miners and other wage laborers, crossed over along with a continuous flow of rural peasants. Unlike earlier decades, women and children began to follow other family members. A circular migration process characterizing immigration of the period prompted notable Mexican American historian George Sanchez to dub the national division between the two countries a "socially-constructed border"; the countries were legally divided, but the border remained permeable until the Great Depression.

The advent of World War I created a labor shortage, which in the West was dominated by agricultural work. The Immigration Act of 1917, which was the first of several early 20th century immigration policies geared specifically at stemming the flow of immigrants, required all those seeking entrance to conform to stringent regulations, including a head tax and a mandatory literacy test. For Mexicans seeking entrance, the new regulations appeared disastrous because many were illiterate peasants. Agricultural business leaders lobbied Congress to take action. That pressure resulted in the first temporary-worker program being issued in 1917. This program allowed Mexicans to come into the United States under a contract lasting until the end of the war. The program was ultimately extended until 1921, resulting in thousands of Mexican workers contracted, primarily in agriculture.

# Background
## Acceptance with Conditions, cont.

The door slammed shut in 1929 once the Great Depression occurred. With the economy in shambles, many Mexican Americans became convenient economic scapegoats, and several hundred thousand were repatriated during the 1930s. States handled repatriation on an individual basis, with such states as California and Texas enacting aggressive campaigns. In all, repatriation reached its height by 1932 but continued through the end of the decade. The emergence of World War II renewed the need for a pliant labor supply.

The impact of World War II was felt on multiple fronts. Not only were workers conscripted into the armed services, but also the internment of thousands of Japanese and Japanese American farmers contributed to a labor shortage. To ameliorate those conditions, the United States and Mexico agreed to a wartime measure, the bilateral Mexican Farm Labor Program or "bracero program", on August 4, 1942. The terms were finalized in 1943. These actions marked the birth of the temporary-worker program aimed at legalizing and regularizing the migrant worker population. Under the bracero program, Mexico allowed its workers to come to the United States for temporary renewable periods under regulated conditions.

As World War II drew to a close, agribusiness lobbied for an extension of the bracero program. The steady inexpensive labor supply allowed agricultural operators to reap many fruits. Without union interference, wages stayed low. In addition, farmers perceived the braceros as an easily managed workforce. Men received contracts while their families remained in Mexico; thus housing costs stayed low. However, the bracero program had social costs. Separation from their families took a toll on Mexican men. In time, some refused to return to Mexico to renew or receive new contracts. Consequently, despite approximately 500,000 contracts issued in 1956 alone, illegal immigration grew alongside the legal work program.

To address the peak in illegal immigration, the Immigration and Naturalization Service launched Operation Wetback. The border patrol, instituted in 1924, was beefed up considerably. In 1954, Operation Wetback nabbed 1.3 million undocumented Mexicans, although some confusion over paperwork resulted in the deportation of a small percentage of legal workers and U.S. citizens. By the end of Operation Wetback in 1957, more than 3.5 million people had been deported. Meanwhile, the bracero program peaked by the mid-1950s.

The bracero program continued largely unchecked until the early 1960s. The program had its critics. Labor unions staunchly opposed the program because it kept wages depressed and other workers seeking farm labor ostensibly locked out of the market. President John F. Kennedy critically reevaluated the program in the early 1960s. The Kennedy administration decided to extend the program only one final year in 1963, citing such consistent abuses as substandard living conditions and depressed wages.

During the late 1960s to the early 1980s, immigration remained largely absent from foreign policy. The Immigration Act of 1965 outlawed the use of national origin quotas, a major provision of the Immigration Act of 1924. Evolving from a series of hearings on illegal immigration beginning in 1971, IRCA aimed at regulating undocumented immigration and provided a "general amnesty" for those who could prove

# Background
## Acceptance with Conditions, cont.

continuous residency in the United States for a minimum of five years before 1982. The Special Agricultural Workers (SAW) provision addressed those who had more recently come to the United States. SAW stipulated that those residing in the United States for at least ninety continuous days during 1985–1986 could receive temporary-resident status. Approximately 1.7 million immigrants and 1.3 million immigrants applied for legalization under general amnesty and SAW, respectively.

President George W. Bush's recent call for a renewed guest-worker program has received a lukewarm reception from both political parties. An extension of temporary visas to potentially millions of undocumented immigrants seeking entrance or those already in the United States has sounded alarms for some within the Republican Party. Senator Jon Kyl, an Arizona Republican and staunch proponent of border control, urged Bush to rethink the immigration plan. Kyl, who heads a subcommittee on terrorism, technology, and homeland security, stated, "Any such legislation must not create opportunities for amnesty, nor confer U.S. citizenship to those who have violated U.S. laws." Democrats, meanwhile, have lodged criticism against a program that they argue does not go far enough to protect immigrant workers. House minority leader Nancy Pelosi, a California Democrat, contends that the proposed program ignores the human costs on immigrant families.

The debate over the guest-worker program is certain to continue, as a recent Gallup poll reveals that 55 percent of Americans disapprove of the proposed immigration plan. Meanwhile, economists argue that the program could boost the ailing economy since low wages would drive down prices of goods and services for consumers.

## MEXICO IN WORLD WAR II

Mexican President Manuel Ávila Camacho followed a strongly pro-
Allied course from the beginning of his administration. After the U.S.
entry into the war in December, 1941, Mexico quickly broke diplomatic
relations with Germany, Japan, and Italy. The Mexican government also
froze Japanese assets and ordered all Axis nationals out of coastal and
defense areas. There was, however, little domestic support for a declaration of war. Mexico did not declare war until German submarines
sank two Mexican oil tankers in May, 1942.

Mexico's involvement in the war meant closer relations with the United
States. Washington wanted bases for U.S. troops in Mexico, whereas
Mexico wanted economic and military aid. The United States never got
the type of base agreement it sought, but there was close cooperation
between the two countries in military matters. Mexico received military
aid under the U.S. lend-lease program, and the two nations established
a joint defense committee to coordinate military activities. Mexico also
established an obligatory military service law, affecting men between
the ages of eighteen and forty-five.

Mexico was one of only two Latin American countries (Brazil being the
other) to furnish combat troops; Mexico provided the 201st Fighter
Squadron, which was equipped with U.S. aircraft and trained in Texas.
The 201st served in the Philippines campaign and had two men killed
in training and five in combat. A more important form of military cooperation was the U.S.–Mexico agreement permitting the United States
to draft Mexican citizens residing in the United States and even to
recruit in Mexico itself. As a result, some 250,000 Mexicans served in
the U.S. armed forces during the war, with 14,000 seeing combat.
Mexican combat veterans received some 1,000 Purple Hearts and one
Medal of Honor.

# Background
## Acceptance with Conditions, cont.

Mexico's greatest contribution to the war was economic. The country provided a variety of strategic materials needed for the war effort: copper, oil, lead, mercury, and zinc. Agricultural products also figured prominently in exports, even though Mexico experienced problems in feeding its own people during the war. Mexico helped to relieve labor shortages in the United States by agreeing to the bracero (day laborer) program, a government-regulated system of contract labor under which Mexican workers found employment in the United States. Originally intended to meet the need for agricultural laborers in the U.S. Southwest, the program was expanded in 1943 to include nonagricultural workers as well. Some 300,000 Mexicans worked under the program during the war years. The war had negative economic consequences for Mexico as well; austerity measures, inflation, and rationing affected the daily lives of its citizens. In June, 1944, the Ávila Camacho administration even suspended the traditional siesta, the afternoon closing of offices and businesses.

World War II had a profound and long-term affect on Mexico's domestic and foreign policies. The war was particularly important in promoting the government's new development approach, with its emphasis on rapid industrialization based on import substitution. The close military ties between Mexico and the United States did not continue after the war, but the already intimate economic connection became even more pronounced. The bracero program—conceived to meet a wartime need—continued until 1964. World War II confirmed and increased the dominant role played by the United States in the Mexican economy.

## THE END OF THE BRACERO PROGRAM (1964)

In response to declining job opportunities, the National Agricultural Workers Union began a vigorous program in 1956 to end the bracero program. In 1958, the Department of Labor improved the standard for bracero housing. In addition, a new formula for determining wages and ensuring a minimum hourly rate was established. As early as 1957, farmers in California began to sense that opposition to the bracero program was mounting and that contract labor was being seriously threatened.

Beginning in 1960, opposition to the bracero program arose in Congress. After acrimonious debate, supporters managed to extend the program for six months. This was the first major attack on the program since its inception in 1942. In 1961, the program was extended another two years, and in 1962, the Kennedy administration openly opposed the program. In 1963, the program was extended a final year only after advocates indicated that the Mexican government strongly opposed an abrupt termination. The Mexican position was that the bracero program functioned as a substitute for illegal immigration.

When the United States unilaterally abolished the bracero program, Mexican officials wanted to reestablish it as a safety valve for growing unemployment. The braceros had acted to help control a growing problem of undocumented immigration. In 1975, Mexico recognized that its attempts to continue the program were unsuccessful and declared that it no longer wanted a workers agreement, that such an agreement had never really succeeded and should not be considered.

# Background
## Acceptance with Conditions, cont.

### THE UNITED STATES AND THE HOME FRONT IN WORLD WAR II

Following its entry into World War II in December, 1941, the United States devoted its considerable resources to the production of industrial goods at previously unimagined levels. This effort allowed the country to become the "arsenal of democracy" envisioned by President Franklin D. Roosevelt. Although the nation's security from direct attack played a considerable role in its remarkable capacity for production, the U.S. achievement was a peculiarly American phenomenon and a function of distinctly American traits.

Still reeling from the effects of the Great Depression, many Americans saw the war as a means to escape hard economic times. In 1940 and 1941, war orders and lend-lease contracts had already begun to bring the nation's economy out of a decade of hardship. The introduction of peacetime conscription removed thousands of young men from the job market, thereby improving job opportunities for those who remained. The military's preparedness campaign also sparked the economy through construction of new military facilities and orders for goods required by the armed services, from tents to aircraft. Grateful for meaningful, well-paying jobs, Americans threw themselves into war work with ardor and energy.

The United States also had three significant underutilized sources for labor on which it could draw. More than six million women entered the workforce. Marginalized by the New Deal programs of the 1930s that had emphasized male breadwinners, many women welcomed the chance to work outside the home. They also embraced the opportunity to make direct contributions to the American war effort, though many worked for unequal wages and were discouraged from joining unions. Most women worked in traditionally female sectors or in newly created industrial jobs, and their share of nonmilitary government jobs nearly doubled during the war. The image of "Rosie the Riveter," sleeves rolled up and bandanna tied in her hair, sent the powerful propaganda message that women in the workforce were crucial to American industrial might.

The United States also called on the labor of African Americans. The combination of Jim Crow segregation in the South and the availability of industrial jobs in the West and North created a "second great migration" (the first occurred during World War I) of nearly 700,000 African Americans from the South. Others moved to industrial and commercial jobs in southern cities such as Atlanta, Montgomery, and New Orleans. African American workers found they could escape racist Jim Crow laws in the North and West, but they continued to face discrimination, lower pay, and outbreaks of white violence. Few of these individuals returned to the South after 1945, however. Some white workers protested the modest advances made by African Americans workers, especially in skilled sectors, and race riots in Detroit and Mobile underscored abiding problems.

Mexicans also helped to solve the nation's need for agricultural labor. The labor crisis caused by the war forced the United States to rethink its immigration policies toward Mexicans. In 1942, the government admitted 200,000 Mexican workers under the bracero program. Untold thousands of other Mexicans entered illegally as immigration restrictions were informally relaxed to meet labor needs. The braceros worked primarily in agriculture in the western states, although they also had jobs in construction and maintenance. The bracero program proved to be so beneficial to the American economy that it was continued into the 1960s.

# Background
## Acceptance with Conditions, cont.

The results of these economic policies were amazing. In 1940, President Roosevelt stunned leaders in the aviation industry by asking them to produce what seemed an impossible goal of 50,000 airplanes; by the end of the war, the United States had produced nearly 300,000. In 1944 alone, the country built 96,318 airplanes, while Germany and Japan together built 67,987. In the same year, the United States built 2,247 major naval vessels; Japan built just 248. By 1944, the United States was producing half of the world's steel. The Ford Motor Company alone produced a greater value of durable goods than did the entire nation of Italy. America's wartime industrial capacity provided the nation tremendous strategic flexibility and allowed the United States to conduct warfare in the European and Pacific theaters simultaneously, while supplying allies such as Britain, the Soviet Union, and China through the lend-lease program.

The massive war production ended a period of chronic unemployment and underemployment in the United States. Job security and high wages meant near universal improvements in American standards of living. Nutrition levels and housing quality increased dramatically, although the concentration of industry in war production meant that many desirable consumer goods, such as automobiles, were hard to find. After its entry into the war, the United States halted production of civilian vehicles. As a consequence, money was available for the purchase of war bonds. Individual savings also rose. Thus, despite being involved in a two-front global war, many people remember World War II as "the good war" in part because of its beneficial effects on the economy.

Relative affluence and a common sense of purpose contributed to a national mood of unity. The war led to a reduction of the divisiveness that had characterized the Depression years.

The persistency of racism notwithstanding, most Americans experienced better economic times and a great deal more optimism in the 1940s than in the 1930s. The sharp contrasts between the war years and the Depression years undoubtedly helped to make the home front a more hopeful place than would have been expected. Government policies that assigned relatively few fathers to combat units helped as well: by sending proportionally fewer fathers into combat, the U.S. military ensured that the nation would have as few widows and orphans as possible. World War II was surely not "the good war" for all Americans, but the U.S. home front did witness dramatic social and economic changes that improved the lives of millions.

# Sources

Ewing, Walter A., "From Denial to Acceptance: Effectively Regulating Immigration to the United States." *Immigration Policy in Focus 3* (Nov. 2004): 3-4; www.ailf.org/ipc/ipf112204.pdf

Miller, E. Willard and Ruby M. Miller, eds. *United States Immigration: A Reference Handbook,* p. 28. Santa Barbara, CA: ABC-CLIO, 1996. http://www.pbs.org/kpbs/theborder/history/timeline/17.html

# Additional Resources

- Using This Resource Book

- Integration into National History Day

- Using ABC-CLIO Websites for Researching Immigration

- Additional Immigration Topic Ideas

# Using This Resource Book

The *Triumph & Tragedy* resource books are designed to provide teachers with all the materials to create interactive lessons centered on a single important topic of American history. In each lesson, the students are asked to analyze primary historical documents and draw conclusions about the topic. You will find two sets of suggested classroom activities in each workbook. For each activity, we have provided background essays, source documents, and reference pieces.

The materials are organized as follows:

## 1. INTRODUCTION

The essay in this section is a broad overview of the resource book's topic. You may use it to create a general lesson or lecture on the issue at hand, or to prepare students for the historical analysis portions.

## 2. THROUGHOUT HISTORY

The material provided here is geared to a specific sub-topic within the broader issue; for example, the role of work in immigration or the legal aspects of free speech. This material may be used to create a preparatory lecture for the resource book's interactive portions, or copied and handed out for the students to read.

## 3A & 3B. DEFINING MOMENTS

Two key historical events are presented in each resource book that illustrate the problems and complex forces at work within each issue. The Defining Moment sections begin with short historical background essays that contextualize the historical event. Again, these pieces may be used to organize a short presentation or given to students to read before beginning the activities.

## 4A & 4B. CLASSROOM ACTIVITY

Each Defining Moment has a Classroom Activity attached. The Activity is broken down into parts, with materials required for each part of the Activity noted. When the Activity calls for Activity Sheets, these are located with the Activity description. In some cases, each portion of the Activity may stand alone, but they are designed to be cumulative. The last part draws on the lessons of the earlier parts, making it the most comprehensive. Some lessons are designed to take up a full class period, some are shorter, and some require homework assignments. The teacher will need to determine what is appropriate for his or her class based upon allotted time and teaching goals.

## 5A & 5B. PRIMARY SOURCES

The historical documents, images, cartoons, etc. called for in the Classroom Activities are in this section, each piece designed to be reproduced for the students. At the end of the Primary Sources are reference sources: glossary words, information on important laws, difficult quotes, background essays, etc. The teacher may wish to make handouts or overheads of this material, or write some of the information on the board to help the students with unfamiliar vocabulary or concepts.

We hope you find this format user-friendly and that you are able to adapt it easily to your students' needs.

# Integration into National History Day

**T**he theme *Triumph and Tragedy in History* is an excellent backdrop for historical research surrounding issues of immigration. As the Chinese and Mexican immigrant stories were presented in this resource book, a picture of individuals with great hope for a better life emerged. Some were triumphant in their quest to become Americans; others endured years of racism and substandard living conditions.

The issues surrounding immigration are complex, interpretative, and relevant; all are excellent qualities of a National History Day research project.

National History Day engages students in historical research. After selecting a topic related to the NHD annual theme, students conduct research into primary and secondary sources. They enter their final projects in competitions using one of four different presentation formats: paper, performance, exhibit, or documentary.

National History Day projects ask students to determine the historical significance of their chosen topics. Projects related to immigration can be approached using different research processes:

- Using primary and secondary documents to tell the story and to place the topic into historical perspective
- Building a timeline of events leading to the conflict to illustrate the significance of the topic
- Presenting an analysis of the conflict through the introduction of the historical context and people involved to deepen historical understanding

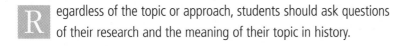 egardless of the topic or approach, students should ask questions of their research and the meaning of their topic in history.

1. Who were the people involved?

2. What were their motivations?

3. Why did the incident occur at this time in history?

4. What was gained and what price was paid?

5. What were the long-term effects of the court case?

Happy researching!

Complete guidelines and more information can be accessed at

**W W W . N H D . O R G**

# Using ABC-CLIO Websites for Researching Immigration

The ABC-CLIO Schools Social Studies Subscription websites combine reference material, curriculum, current events, and primary sources in a single resource to help make historical research straightforward, accessible, and exciting for students. They provide students with the tools they need to investigate and assess the important questions associated with the topic of immigration. Questions to consider include:

Why has immigration played such an important role in the history of the United States?

Why do immigrants come to the United States? Are newcomers always welcomed? Why or why not?

What are the difficulties associated with immigration?

How have attitudes toward immigrants and immigration in the United States changed over time?

With these websites, students can find entries related to the topic of immigration that link to related reference and primary source material, providing historical context that will help students develop their skills of source evaluation and historical analysis. Teachers can construct customized research lists of reference entries, images, maps, and documents, enabling students to compare, contrast, and analyze a variety of related resources.

## ABC-CLIO's social studies subscription websites:

- Provide students access to deeper and broader content than other social studies resources, allowing students to synthesize what they learn from reference material and primary sources
- Combine reference, curriculum, and current events, which are updated daily
- Are correlated to curriculum standards, key assessments, and major textbooks
- Meet the needs of students for different grade levels and assignments
- Provide access from school and home for students and faculty

# Additional Immigration Topic Ideas

1. Cultures Collide: Immigration of the North Africans into Spain

2. The Hmong in Wisconsin: A new ingredient in the melting pot

3. Arab Immigration to France

4. African American Immigration to Liberia

5. Closing the Door: The Immigration Act of 1924

6. Asian Pineapple: Japanese laborers in Hawaii

7. Ellis Island or Angel Island: A symbol of immigration

8. Americanizing the Masses: Factory classrooms in the industrial age

9. Forcing Loyalty: The pledge of allegiance

10. Why We Came Here: Stories of immigration from generation to generation

11. Braving the Wind: The Swedish immigrants on the Great Plains

12. Holding Back the Hordes: Literacy tests and immigration obstacles

13. Jane Addams and Hull House: Assimilating the immigrant

14. Immigration and Nationality Act 1952

15. Refugee Act of 1980

16. Angel Island: Paper sons and daughters

17. Japanese Picture Brides Marry into America

18. Who is an Acceptable Immigrant: Defining legal aliens

19. First Generation: Caught between culture and citizenship

20. Doing the Dirty Work: Taking the jobs Americans won't